CHARTISM

Eric J Evans
Series editor: Christopher Culpin

Longman

CONTENTS

PART ONE

INTRODUCTION

Chartism was a political movement of the late 1830s and 1840s. Although some members of the middle classes supported it and many of its leaders were well educated and reasonably prosperous, it was in essence a movement of working people. 'Chartists' were given this name because they supported the **People's Charter**. This document's 'Six Points' called for government to be run on the principles of democracy, or rather 'adult-male democracy', because the charter specifically did not call for 'votes for women'.

KEY TERMS

Universal suffrage and **universal manhood suffrage** – these terms literally mean the vote for everyone and the vote for all men. In practice, the Chartists did propose some restrictions to the adult-male suffrage (see page 9).

The **People's Charter** was drawn up in the form of a petition to parliament calling for the establishment of a democratic system of government. It contained six points (see page 9).

Nevertheless, in the context of the time, the Chartists were calling for a huge change in the political system, which was controlled by a small and very wealthy group of people, mostly titled landowners or aristocrats. Many opponents of Chartism called it 'revolutionary' and pledged to oppose it by all means possible.

In your initial survey of the events which are outlined in this chapter, think about the following lines of enquiry.
- **What caused working people to protest so vigorously and so consistently for political change?**
- **What did Chartists believe?**

◢ Was Chartism just a movement of economically depressed workers?

◢ Was Chartism really a national movement, or just a series of outbreaks in different parts of Britain?

◢ Can Chartism be seen as an expression of working-class solidarity against other social groups which were hostile to them?

◢ Chartism did not achieve its famous 'Six Points'. Does this mean that it was a failure overall?

Chronology of important events

1789   French Revolution breaks out. Many skilled workers in Britain are enthused by its example and call for parliamentary reform on the basis of 'one man, one vote'

1790s   Artisan radical movements emerge in Britain, with similar objectives to those of the Chartists more than 40 years later. The government of William Pitt passes laws against radical meetings

1815–20   Re-emergence of political radicalism, with mass protests against the government in many parts of the country

1819   In the so-called Peterloo Massacre, a local force in Manchester kills a number of people assembled at a peaceful meeting calling for parliamentary reform. The Peterloo Massacre creates martyrs for the cause of reform and puts the government of Lord Liverpool on the defensive

1829–32   Reform Act crisis leads to passage of the 'Great' Reform Act which extends the vote but not to working people. Over the next 20 years, the size of electorates in many parliamentary constituencies actually declines

1834   The Poor Law Amendment Act introduces a new principle of 'less eligibility' designed to make application for relief against poverty as degrading as possible. It is hotly opposed by many working people, especially in the industrial north of England

1835   Working men's and radical associations are formed in Scotland and parts of the north of England

1836   Newspaper Act passed. It reduces stamp duty (tax) on papers to 1*d* for each edition of a newspaper. Many working-class leaders complain that there should be no 'taxes on knowledge' at all

London Working Men's Association formed (June); National Radical Association of Scotland formed (August)

1837   East London Democratic Association founded. Various other radical associations formed, especially in the textile districts of Lancashire and Yorkshire, to protest against the New Poor Law. First appearance of the most popular, and influential, Chartist newspaper *Northern Star* (November)

1838   Formation of London Democratic Association by George Julian Harney, as a more popular rival to the London Working Men's Association (March) Publication of the People's Charter and the National Chartist Petition (May). Mass rallies and meetings held throughout the country, such as that held at Kersal Moor (September)

1839   First Chartist National Convention, the General Convention of the Industrious Classes, meets in London (February), then transfers to Birmingham (May); riots in Birmingham's Bull Ring (July)

National Chartist Petition rejected by the House of Commons (235 votes to 46) (July); demonstrations and mass meetings; arrests of leading Chartists begin, but few are held for more than 18 months

An attempted rising of working people in Newport (Monmouthshire) is defeated (November)

1840   Attempted people's risings in Sheffield and Bradford (Yorkshire) (January)

A number of Chartists are brought to trial (February/March)

Chartist conference meets in Manchester (July) and forms the National Charter Association, attempting to reunite the movement; local areas nominate members to a general council

1841   More support for Chartism builds up as trade depression has its effect but many divisions are apparent between leaders and over tactics

Foundation of the National Association by William Lovett (April) – seen as a more moderate rival to the National Charter Association

National Charter Association agrees to present another petition (September)

1842   Formation of the Complete Suffrage Movement by Joseph Sturge – an attempt to unite the interests of middle-class and working-class supporters of radical reform (January)

Chartist National Convention meets in London (April)

House of Commons decides by 287 votes to 49 not even to consider the second Chartist petition (May)

Chartists support strikes and other forms of direct industrial action, including sabotaging boilers (the Plug Plot riots) (August); close co-operation between trade unions and Chartists at local level; further arrests of Chartist leaders; trials begin in October

1843   Feargus O'Connor tried in Lancaster (March) on charges of seditious conspiracy; convicted of minor charges and released

Chartist National Convention accepts a plan supported by Feargus O'Connor for land reform (September). This aims to buy up plots of land and settle Chartists on them in democratic communities. Those wanting land put their names forward and are drawn by ballot

1844   National Charter Association convention meets in Manchester (April)

Northern Star begins publication from London (November)

1845   At the National Charter Association convention in London the Chartist Land Co-Operative Society is established (April)

1846   Land bought for Chartist colonies at Heronsgate (Hertfordshire) and Lowbands (Worcestershire)

1847   First Chartist land colony opened at Heronsgate (near Rickmansworth, Hertfordshire). It was named O'Connorville (May)

Chartist Land Co-Operative Society changes its name to National Co-Operative Land Company

1848   Riots in London, Manchester and Glasgow (March)

Chartist National Convention held in London (April) and demonstration held on Kennington Common, south London (April); authorities do not allow a petition to be presented by a large body of Chartists; O'Connor and a small delegation deliver it to parliament; after threats of violence, the meeting on Kennington common breaks up peacefully: the last substantial Chartist assembly

Further riots in London (May/June)

Land colonies at Snig's End (Gloucestershire) and Minster Lovell – otherwise known as Charterville – (Oxfordshire) opened

1849   New Chartist journal *Democratic Review* set up, edited by George Julian Harney

Great Dodford (Worcestershire) land colony established

1850   Bronterre O'Brien's National Reform League founded (January); O'Connor's grip on Chartist leadership begins to weaken

1851   National Co-Operative Land Company (formerly the Chartist Land Co-Operative Society) wound up (August)

Divisions within the National Charter Association on the best way forward for the Chartists leads to resignation of the more militant Ernest Jones and George Julian Harney (December)

1852   George Julian Harney and Ernest Jones in effective control of what remains of Chartism

Last issue of *Northern Star* (March)

O'Connor declared insane (June)

1858   Last Chartist National Convention held; it agrees on co-operation with moderate radicals in a Political Reform League to press for further parliamentary reform (February)

From this long list of events, you should be able to work out a number of things about Chartism. Among the most important are the following:

1 The ideas which came to a climax as Chartism were not at all new.

2 Even during the 1830s and 1840s, when it posed the greatest threat to the authorities, Chartism had peaks and troughs. The main 'peaks' took place in 1838–39, 1841–42 and 1848. Chartism never recovered as a genuinely popular mass movement from the major defeat it suffered in 1848.

3 Chartism was a genuinely national movement, although it was much stronger in some areas than in others.

4 Chartism alarmed the authorities enough for them to respond by arresting Chartist leaders during the main periods of agitation. Government reaction, however, was usually measured and considered. It had no interest in executing Chartists, which would have created martyrs to the cause.

5 A number of plans were made for a general uprising of Chartists to take control of the country by force, although few of them amounted to much. For some, Chartism was a genuinely revolutionary movement.

6 Chartism was capable of uniting a very large number of working people in support of the cause of democracy. Disagreements between leaders about tactics were, however, frequent.

The 'Six Points' of the People's Charter (May 1838)

The 'Six Points'	Comment
1 The vote for all adult males	*Voters must be 21 years or over and 'a native of these realms'. The vote was NOT to be given to those 'convicted of a felony' or to those declared insane*
2 Payment for members of parliament	*'Be it enacted, that every Member of the House of Commons . . . be paid £500 per annum'. As the committee which drafted the 'Six Points' explained, the salary would enable 'an honest tradesman, or working man . . . to serve a constituency, when taken from his business to attend to the interests of the country'*
3 Each parliamentary constituency should have roughly the same number of voters	*'Be it enacted, that for the purpose of obtaining an equal representation of the people in the Commons House of Parliament, the United Kingdom be divided into 300 electoral districts . . . that each district contain, as nearly as may be, an equal number of inhabitants'*
4 Voting should be by secret ballot	*'. . . electors to vote only in the district in which they are registered; voting to be by secret ballot'*
5 No property qualification: that is, members of parliament should not be required to have property before being allowed to sit in parliament	*'That no other qualification shall be required for members to serve in the Commons House of Parliament, than the choice of the electors'*
6 General elections to be held once a year	*Election of members of parliament to take place in June each year*

Comments on the People's Charter

A number of things are worth noting about the People's Charter.

◢ It was a highly political document; none of its terms had to do with wages, conditions of work or the economy.

◢ It reflected the priorities of the informed and literate *artisan radicals* who had been parliamentary reformers for at least a generation.

KEY TERMS

Artisans were skilled workers. Most had served a long apprenticeship and usually had regular work with wages higher than those of most workers. Artisans who had lost their status and earning power were among the strongest supporters of Chartism.

Radical – according to the literal definition, radicals wanted to get to the root of things. Having done so, they wanted significant change, usually to improve their social and political position. In the context of the late eighteenth and early nineteenth centuries, many radicals were influenced by the ideas of the European Enlightenment, wanting a large extension in the number of people able to vote. Not all radicals believed the same things, however.

◢ It can be read as a commentary on what these artisan radicals, following William Cobbett, were inclined to call 'old corruption'. This was the system, built up during the eighteenth century, by which landowners would use their wealth and power to get their way, often by buying support. Voting in public could also lead to intimidation and undesirable 'influence'. After 1832, when tenant farmers were able to vote in the rural areas, there was substantial evidence that landowners paid close attention to how their tenants voted. Some were threatened with eviction unless they voted according to the landowner's preference. Annual parliaments were proposed to make it too costly for powerful people to buy political privilege.

◢ The proposal to pay members of parliament a salary was most obviously a way of ensuring that working men could afford to sit in parliament, but also a way of reducing the influence of landowners who frequently put forward their own nominees (often members of their own families) as members. Many in the middle classes could not afford to absent themselves from work either, so this proposal was designed to give more influence to those whom radicals called members of the 'productive classes' (*i.e.* those who increased the nation's wealth) and to reduce that of the 'non-productive classes' (*i.e.* those whose income derived not from work, or from taking the risks in producing or selling things, but from the rent they charged for tenants to farm their lands. Rent was widely considered by radicals to be 'unearned income').

Chartism unfolds: a narrative

The list of important events above provides a basic chronology of the nineteenth century's most significant popular movement, Chartism. A brief narrative of its main phases will help to make more sense of the thematic chapters which follow.

1837–40

Pressure for further political reform had been building up in three main areas:

1 London, the traditional centre of radical activity and the home of the new London Working Men's Association

2 the industrial north of England, particularly south-east Lancashire and west Yorkshire. Here opposition to the implementation of the New Poor Law was both fierce and persistent

3 central Scotland, where a number of new radical associations were founded in 1835–36. In August 1839, most of these came together in a new Universal Suffrage Central Committee for Scotland.

A national convention, as an alternative and more democratic assembly to parliament, was proposed during 1838 and Chartist lecturers toured the country persuading mass meetings of its value and calling for nominations. The first Chartist National Convention, to which 53 delegates had been nominated, met in London in February 1839. By no means all of these were working people, and Figure 1 conveys the clear impression of a well-ordered gathering of respectable folk.

The National Chartist Petition, containing almost 1.3 million signatures, was presented to parliament in May 1839 but Chartists could not agree on what action to take if it were rejected. Even before parliament

SMYTH

threw it out in July, violence was threatening. Reports came in to the authorities that people were arming themselves and drilling, especially on the moorlands of Lancashire and Yorkshire. They responded by attempting to ban large meetings, but with little success. Arrests quickly followed, especially after a riot in Birmingham's Bull Ring in July. By the end of the summer most of the Chartist leaders were under arrest, together with a large number of the rank and file.

Rejection of the National Chartist Petition provoked open defiance and rebellion in south Wales in November 1839 when about seven thousand colliers and iron workers marched on Newport (Monmouthshire) led by John Frost. The intention was to begin a full-scale rebellion throughout south Wales but the attack was beaten off by soldiers, with the loss of more than twenty lives. Frost and other leaders were sentenced to death, but the sentences were commuted. Frost was eventually transported for 16 years. Further attempts at rebellion took place in south Yorkshire in January 1840 and provoked more arrests. Almost six hundred Chartists were imprisoned between 1838 and 1841.

Chartist leadership was divided between 1839 and 1840 and the National Charter Association, founded in Manchester in July 1840, was an attempt (masterminded by O'Connor from York gaol) to unify and revive its fortunes.

1841–42

Support for the National Charter Association grew between 1840 and 1841, especially in the industrial areas of northern England. After O'Connor's release from prison in 1841, Chartists began to call for another convention and the presentation of a fresh petition to parliament. The details were orchestrated by the National Charter Association against a background of increasing industrial distress. This organisation, which claimed to have more than fifty thousand members by the end of the year, elected delegates to the convention which met in April 1842. The delegates comprised a much larger proportion of working people than in 1839. Few Chartists supported the attempt made in Birmingham by the Quaker merchant Joseph Sturge to bring

Figure 1 Engraving of the first Chartist National Convention in session

about, through his Complete Suffrage Movement, what the nonconformist leader Edward Miall called a 'reconciliation between the middle and lower classes'.

Popular unrest was heightened by the death in prison of the young Sheffield Chartist Samuel Holberry in June 1842. The key development of the summer, however, was the severe industrial unrest which spread through much of Scotland, northern England and the English midlands. The catalyst was wage-cutting – first, apparently, by colliery owners in Longton (Staffordshire) in June. Employers in the textile areas of Stalybridge and Ashton-under-Lyne (Cheshire), followed suit in August, well aware that workers were being invited, as the factory inspector Leonard Horner noted, to take 'employment on any terms, or starvation'. Chartists supported the strikes and industrial sabotage which broke out, but they did not initiate these actions.

The lead was taken by trade unions who nevertheless supported the People's Charter. The strikes did not last long but, accompanied by violence which included arson and destruction of houses in Staffordshire and attacks on troops attempting to keep order in west Yorkshire, they presented one of the biggest challenges to authority of the nineteenth century. Arrests once again followed. In Staffordshire, for example, a special commission was established to try 274 Chartists, resulting in wholesale imprisonment and some transportation. The well-publicised trial of O'Connor (following his arrest in 1842) was only the tip of the iceberg; in Lancashire and Cheshire hundreds were imprisoned for short periods.

Though the challenges of 1842 were extensive, the authorities were well equipped to meet them. Troops could be moved quickly and efficiently by train. The government had learned not to over-react and a good harvest alleviated some of the grinding misery of working people. Meanwhile, as trade finally revived, employers quietly rescinded the wage cuts they had imposed earlier in the year. Some Chartist leaders felt that they had lost control of events. Certainly, trade disruption and massive industrial unrest had brought the People's Charter no nearer to realisation.

1847–48

Chartist activity in 1848 needs to be seen against a background of failed harvests and rises in food prices across Europe. The devastating famine in Ireland (1845–47) was a peculiarly acute symptom of a more widespread disease and the year 1848 was known as a year of revolutions in Europe. *Northern Star* celebrated this joyfully.

◢ Source

Glory to the Proletarians of Paris, they have saved the Republic.

The work goes bravely on. Germany is revolutionised from end to end ...

How long, Men of Great Britain and Ireland, how long will you carry the damning stigma of being the only people who dare not will their freedom.

Patience! the hour is nigh! From the hill-tops of Lancashire, from the voices of hundreds of thousands has ascended to heaven the oath of union, and the rallying cry of conflict.

Englishmen and Irishmen have sworn to have THE CHARTER AND REPEAL *or* VIVE LA REPUBLIQUE *[long live the republic].*

Northern Star, 25 March 1848, quoted in
E. Royle, **Chartism** (Addison Wesley Longman, 1996)

As mass support dwindled after 1842, such unity as Chartism had been able to maintain had come from *Northern Star*, the leadership of O'Connor and the undeniable attractions of what amounted to a Chartist 'national lottery' through his land plan to secure a couple of acres on which Chartists could start a new life in the countryside. Links had also been maintained with nationalists in Ireland, incensed by the catastrophe engulfing their country. By late 1847, O'Connor, now a member of parliament, harboured what he believed to be genuine hopes for the cause of liberty.

The early months of 1848 did seem to afford some hope. Chartist speakers attracted comfortingly large crowds. High food prices in March brought rioting crowds onto the streets of Glasgow and a Poor Law workhouse was attacked in Manchester. Delegates were elected to attend a third Chartist National Convention in early April. News of the fall of King Louis Philippe in France led some property owners in Britain to fear a revolution, not least when they heard news of the mass meeting summoned by the Chartists to be held on Kennington Common on 10 April.

The government of Lord John Russell, like that of Sir Robert Peel almost six years earlier, remained calm. Its reaction, however, was hardly muted. It put 8 000 troops on alert and recruited 85 000 special constables to keep order. It put the now 78-year-old Duke of Wellington (the victor at the Battle of Waterloo almost thirty-three years earlier) in symbolic charge of the main garrison in London. Crucially, the home secretary, Sir George Grey, took the decision to ban a projected march from Kennington Common to Westminster. The march was to accompany the delivery of a fresh Chartist petition, which O'Connor claimed would have five million signatures.

O'Connor was allowed to make his address to the several thousand (perhaps as many as 50 000) who assembled on Kennington Common but he was required to present his petition peacefully, accompanied by only a small group of followers. He complied. Though Russell gleefully reported that the Chartist adventure had 'proved a complete failure', he was aware of plans elsewhere, including Manchester, to continue the struggle. The Chartist National Convention continued to meet for a while, although its purpose was unclear after the House of Commons ridiculed a petition which was discovered to have fewer than two million signatures, and to include a large number of false names upon it.

Nevertheless, despite much relieved ridicule by the propertied classes, some kind of Chartist threat remained into the summer of 1848 when the troops had to restore order in Bradford after the police had failed to do so, and the police had to break up meetings in London's East End. Spies infiltrated plans for armed rising in Lancashire in August and averted trouble. As in 1839 and 1842, the restoring of order was accompanied by a substantial number of arrests. Ernest Jones spent two years in prison. Although the movement limped on for another decade, its power to bring the masses on to the streets ended in the summer of 1848.

Figure 2 Photograph of Chartists assembled on Kennington Common on 10 April 1848

Feargus O'CONNOR *1794–1855*

Feargus O'Connor was the most high profile, charismatic and controversial of the Chartist leaders. He was not a working man, coming from a family of Irish landowners, and was educated in Dublin as a lawyer. He was member of parliament for Cork from 1832 to 1835 when he supported the Irish nationalist Daniel O'Connell; later they became bitter enemies because of O'Connell's support for the new poor law and his attacks on direct action by working men. O'Connor emerged as the most powerful Chartist leader from the early 1840s, using *Northern Star*, of which he was effectively the owner, to publish not only his own views but those of others. He did not edit the paper but wrote a front-page 'letter' each week. His journal, selling as many as 50 000 copies a week at its peak, kept Chartists in different parts of the country in touch with events nationwide. O'Connor made many enemies among other leading Chartists and historical opinion is divided as to the value of his contribution. He was widely accused of arrogance and of being a 'rabble-rouser'. William Lovett spoke contemptuously of his habit, after release from gaol in 1841, of speaking to Chartist crowds in a fustian (coarse cotton) suit, symbolising his solidarity with the working classes and 'the blistered hands and fustian jackets of Manchester'. Many of those who worked most closely with him, like George Julian Harney, however, were warm in their praise. He was a powerful, though not a subtle, orator. One journalist, reporting a speech made in Carlisle in 1838, noted that the printed word 'could give but a faint idea of the effect of Mr O'Connor's address upon the meeting'. Some objected that his speeches, full as one said of 'bombast, broken metaphor and inflated language' raised unrealistic expectations in unsophisticated audiences.

In Chartism's later years, O'Connor championed the land plan (see Chronology of important events on page 7 and Chapter 4). This raised yet more controversy. Other leaders argued that Chartists should be more concerned with improving the conditions of industrial workers than in romantic schemes to put them back on the land. He became the only Chartist member of parliament when he was returned for Nottingham in the 1847 election. He died insane in an asylum.

Thomas COOPER *1805–92*

Thomas Cooper trained as a shoemaker in Leicester. Early in the Chartist period, he was a strong supporter of Feargus O'Connor but broke with him in the mid-1840s, calling him 'a rash and vindictive man'. He produced a string of radical journals in the midlands, notably the *Midland Counties Illuminator* (1841), *The Chartist Advocate*

(1842) and *Cooper's Journal* (1850), wonderfully subtitled *Unfettered Thinker and Plain Speaker for Truth, Freedom and Progress*. He was imprisoned for two years (1843–45) for his part in the Plug Plot riots. Then he had called for 'a physical force struggle … We must get the people out to fight; and they must be irresistible, if they were united', a position he later regretted. He steered clear of the 1848 riots, noting in his autobiography, *Life of Thomas Cooper*: 'Experience has rendered me a little wiser than to suffer myself to be mixed up in any plot.' He established an adult evening and Sunday school in Leicester. His later career was as a writer on the fringes of literary circles. His autobiography is one of the main sources for students of Chartism.

George Julian HARNEY *1817–97*

George Julian Harney was born in Deptford (London) and brought up in humble circumstances. He was a cabin boy on ship before working as a barman in London. Here he became associated with Henry Hetherington and, like him, resented the strong middle-class links which the London Working Men's Association had developed. In response, the East London Democratic Association was formed. During a speech on Newcastle-upon-Tyne's Town Moor in May 1839, he provided a clear focus for resistance: 'Let them [the working men] be determined to have their rights, peaceably if they could, forcibly if they must.' Privately, however, he did not believe that

revolution could succeed. During the 1840s, under the influence of Friedrich Engels, he became more interested in European republicanism and socialism. He was editor of *Northern Star* from 1845 to 1850 where increasingly he developed socialist sympathies. He argued in the paper in 1848 that 'political institutions are merely to be regarded as the *means* to an end … especially … the happiness, prosperity and independence … of that class whose labour produces the wealth of the country.' He broke with Feargus O'Connor in 1850 and began to edit a new socialist journal *Red Republican*. After 1852, however, when he also fell out with Ernest Jones, both his socialist and his European interests waned and he drifted back to British republicanism, which flourished briefly in the 1860s.

Henry HETHERINGTON *1792–1849*

Henry Hetherington trained as a printer before becoming one of the most impressive working-class journalists of the century. As proprietor of *Poor Man's Guardian* in the 1830s, he led the campaign against taxes on newspapers – 'the war of the unstamped' – which enjoyed partial success in 1836. He was one of the six members of the London Working Men's Association who, with six members of parliament led by Daniel O'Connell, drafted a version of the People's Charter in June 1837. He toured Yorkshire as a London Working Men's Association representative in 1837, urging workers to form their own provincial associations. As the early Chartist historian Gammage noted, he was no orator: 'He was not the man for those impulsive beings upon whom solid argument is lost, but whose souls are stirred to their depths by fiery declamation; but was rather adapted to the intelligent and the thoughtful.' His base remained London, where he attempted to revive democratic agitation when he founded the Metropolitan Charter Union in April 1840. Totally opposed to the style and flamboyance of Feargus O'Connor, he played little part in Chartism during the 1840s. His early work, however, represents one of the strongest, and most honoured, links between London artisan radicalism and Chartism.

Ernest JONES *1819–69*

Ernest Jones was one of the youngest of the national Chartist leaders, and by some way the most privileged in terms of birth. He was the son of a colonel who had served as equerry to the Duke of Cumberland. Jones trained in London as a lawyer, though he was also an accomplished poet and wrote many effective verses. He joined the Chartist movement in 1846 under the patronage of Feargus O'Connor and, like him, remained a strong supporter of the land plan. He was elected the representative of Halifax, in west Yorkshire, for the Chartist National Convention held in London in April 1848 and was arrested in June, remaining in prison for two years. He became the most clearly socialist of all the Chartist leaders and when he led the movement in its last years after 1852, he made it clear that he opposed not only rich 'landlords' and 'moneylords' but also those skilled workers who were organising themselves into trade unions. In his *Notes to the People* (1852) he called unions 'a perfect fallacy' and suggested to the highly paid iron workers that 'the low-paid trades sympathise not with the haughty aristocracy of labour that has spurned them ... there is aristocratic privilege of the vilest die among the high-paid trades, and we ought to fight against it too.' He also opposed the co-operative movement: 'Co-operation cannot be carried out successfully, without first obtaining the political rights of the people.' He tried to maintain the viability of Chartism into the 1850s. After 1848, however, although pockets of effective organisation survived in Staffordshire and west Yorkshire, Chartism ceased to be a national movement. Jones acknowledged defeat in 1858 when he called a conference which established the Political Reform League, an organisation which linked the Chartism remnant to middle-class radicals to achieve further parliamentary reform. In the general election of 1868, he won 10 000 votes standing as a 'Lib-Lab' radical candidate.

William LOVETT *1800–77*

William Lovett was born in Cornwall. He arrived in London in 1821, training as a cabinet maker. With Henry Hetherington and James Watson he helped form the National Union of the Working Classes in 1831 at the height of the Reform Act crisis. He also campaigned with them to remove taxes on newspapers and was one of the founders of the London Working Men's Association in 1836. A true organisation of educated skilled workers, the London Working Men's Association aimed 'to draw into one bond of unity the intelligent and influential portion of the working classes in town and country'. With the veteran radical member of parliament Francis Place, he drafted the People's Charter which was presented to parliament in 1838. His emphasis on 'improving' the working classes by encouraging education and temperate habits, his close links with middle-class radicals and his evident preference for 'moral force' all distanced him from James Bronterre O'Brien and Feargus O'Connor. Like most other Chartists he was arrested in 1839 and, while imprisoned in Warwick gaol, wrote with John Collins *Chartism: A New Organisation for the People*. This called for a national education system to be paid for by a 'tax' of 1*d* a week on all who had signed the Chartist petition. Lovett became ever more convinced that 'it is the ignorance of our brethren which generates and fosters despots' and continued to campaign for the working classes to acquire more knowledge, making them worthy to receive the vote. His National Association for the Moral, Social and Political Improvement of the People (1841) was fiercely attacked by O'Connor as weakening the thrust of the National Charter Association. Lovett was little more than a fringe figure within Chartism after

1841. However, his work, combined with that of 'moral-force' (see Chapter 3) Chartists like Henry Vincent who called for 'teetotal Chartism', contributed much to a 'culture of improvement' warmly embraced by many respectable working people and welcomed by many in the governing classes. It was at the heart of radical Liberalism during the 1850s and 1860s and, arguably, achieved more than Chartism did. He was one of a number of Chartists to write an autobiography on which historians have relied. Its full title gives a very clear idea of his priorities: *The Life and Struggles of William Lovett in his pursuit of Bread, Knowledge and Freedom*.

James Bronterre O'BRIEN *1805–64*

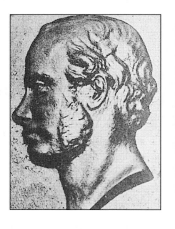

James Bronterre O'Brien was born in Ireland and trained as a lawyer before coming to Britain and participating with Henry Hetherington in the campaign against taxes on newspapers. He was one of the deepest thinkers in the movement. Feargus O'Connor called him 'the schoolmaster of Chartism' and his grasp of theoretical issues impressed Friedrich Engels. He had worked with Hetherington and George Julian Harney on 'the war of the unstamped' (campaign against taxes on newspapers) in the mid-1830s and he edited *Poor Man's Guardian*. His journals *Bronterre's National Reformer* (1837) and *Operative* (1838–39) helped to spread the Chartist message before *Northern Star* (for which he also wrote until 1841) became established. He worked closely with O'Connor for a time but fell out with him in 1841, after which he became increasingly isolated. He was one of the few national leaders to develop links with Joseph Sturge's Complete Suffrage Movement in 1842 and this lost him credibility with many. He believed, as he said in *The English Chartist Circular* in 1841, that 'the grand evil of society' lay 'not in private property, but in the unjust and atrocious powers with which the existing laws of all countries invest it' and that 'The employers of labour and the exchangers of wealth are alone considered in the laws. The producers … are only thought of as slaves or criminals.' He resigned from the National Charter Association in 1848 and his followers in London provide a long-term link with the emergence of a separate Labour party.

PART TWO

CHAPTER ONE

WHY DID CHARTISM EMERGE AS A MASS MOVEMENT?

Objectives

◢ To understand the roots of Chartism
◢ To examine why so many people supported it
◢ To show the differences between long-term and short-term causes.

Origins and long-term causes

You can see from the chronology of important events in the Introduction that Chartism was a mass movement during the late 1830s and the 1840s. Since it takes its name from the People's Charter, which was published in 1838, you might think that the ideas which the Chartists believed in were new. In fact, all of the 'Six Points' (see page 9) had been on the political agenda for at least half a century.

Probably the best way to understand the significance of the movement is to appreciate that it emerged towards the end of a long period of agitation by political outsiders. People had been agitating for some kind of parliamentary reform since the 1760s. Though agitation for political change was very strong at some times (especially the late 1760s, late 1770s, 1790s, 1815–20 and 1829–32) and much weaker at others, skilled workers in London and other large towns had been calling for a large increase in the numbers of people entitled to elect members of parliament for more than half a century before Chartism was born. After the outbreak of the French Revolution in 1789, the number of people involved in agitation to produce substantial changes in voting rights and parliamentary representation increased considerably. Thomas Paine (1737–1809) produced a book entitled *Rights of Man* in 1791–92. This book stated that citizens had the right to pass judgement on their governors, and get rid of them if they did not like what they were doing. The civilised, peaceful way to do this was by an election. Paine called for all men to be able to vote in such elections.

Paine's book was extremely effective. Its impact alarmed the authorities. Here is the view of William Pitt the younger, then prime minister, talking in parliament in 1794 about the impact of the new radical societies which had been so much influenced by it. These societies wanted:

◢ Source 1

... [a] whole system of insurrection ... laid in the modern doctrine of the rights of man; – that monstrous doctrine, under which the weak and ignorant, who are most susceptible of impression from [most likely to be influenced by] such barren, abstract positions, were attempted to be seduced to overturn government, law, security, property, religion, order and everything valuable in this country ...

William Pitt the Younger, House of Commons, 1794

Perhaps the prime minister was right to show alarm. Paine had converted thousands of working men to his way of thinking, which had itself been influenced by ideas of the so-called European Enlightenment in the second half of the eighteenth century and by the French Revolution. Paine took part in this revolution. Since so many of his most loyal readers were craftsmen and artisans, Paine is often said to have started off a period of 'artisan radicalism'. Though few were revolutionaries, artisan radicals, working in 'corresponding societies', challenged the authorities' right to govern and tried to persuade people of the need for a complete change in the system of government. On many occasions between 1789 and 1832, reformers were able to persuade thousands of working people to attend mass meetings which passed resolutions calling for the changes they wanted. During this period, all of the ideas which eventually appeared in the People's Charter were regularly discussed.

You can see, then, that the origins of Chartism go back a long way. One of the central tasks of an historian is to look for the causes of major events. These causes can nearly always be divided into 'long-term' and 'short-term' causes. It is not the task of this book to develop the longer term causes of Chartism in detail. However, the following items give some indication of the long-term issues involved in explaining why Chartism emerged:

◢ A long period of considerable change during which the social groups ruling Britain hardly changed at all. Britain was ruled by aristocrats and large landowners throughout the eighteenth and early nineteenth centuries. Did Britain's rulers at the end of the eighteenth century adequately represent (or even understand) the lives of the people over whom they ruled?

◢ Major changes in society were brought about by an industrial revolution which got under way in the second half of the eighteenth century. That revolution created new forms of wealth, particularly in factory towns and ports. Many of the towns which were creating so much of Britain's new wealth – Manchester, Birmingham, Leeds, Sheffield, etc. – could not elect their own members of parliament.

◢ The people entitled to vote for members of parliament were very restricted in number and there was little consistency in their qualifications. In a very few towns, like Coventry or Northampton, rights to vote were very wide. Something close to male democracy existed there. In far more places, however, voting rights were very restricted. Most parliamentary constituencies had fewer than 200 voters.

◢ New ideas about government were being discussed in Europe. Thomas Paine and his book *Rights of Man* made them much more popular in Britain in the 1790s. He made thousands of working people politically aware – and anxious for change. Increasingly, they talked about 'citizenship' and about 'political rights', especially 'the Rights of Man'.

◢ The industrial revolution made successful factory owners, businessmen and financiers very wealthy. However, economic growth was very jerky. There were periods when the new industries were in depression. At such times – the 1790s, 1815–20 and 1829–32 stand out – pressure for change in the political system increased substantially. People who were out of work, or facing higher food prices, or both, expressed discontent with their rulers and called for change.

◢ The industrial revolution produced many long-term casualties.

Among these were people who did not work in factories. The majority of working people at the time of Chartism were not factory workers. Skilled workers whose skills were no longer needed, or who found themselves increasingly in competition with more modern forms of production, tended to be particularly hard hit. The biggest group in this category was that of handloom weavers. Many were both literate and highly informed politically. They usually worked on the fringes of the main areas of industry, in so-called 'industrial villages' rather than in the largest towns. They were found in the villages and small towns of the Pennines, such as Todmorden on the Lancashire-Yorkshire border, or Sabden in east Lancashire. Others were concentrated in parts of the country which were being by-passed by the industrial revolution with its need for efficient communications, first by canal and later by railway. Some of the strongest support for Chartism came from previously prosperous weaving areas, such as Trowbridge and Melksham in Wiltshire. So when the conditions for handloom weavers worsened, as they did rapidly once the mechanised power loom became entrenched in the main centres of production from the middle of the 1820s, they became more than depressed economically. They also had the burning sense that a wrong had been done to them by a productive process which threatened not only their wages but their entire way of life. Handloom weavers looked to Chartism to defend an entire political and social culture. It is not surprising that they became its most numerous supporters during the late 1830s and early 1840s, providing much the largest single occupational group at the first Chartist National Convention in 1839 (see page 6).

People who struggled to make ends meet had been taught by Paine, and the writers, journalists and lecturers who followed him, to believe that the real cause of their misery was 'misgovernment'. Radicals like Henry ('Orator') Hunt and William Cobbett used both mass meetings and newspapers to develop their argument that a parliament which did not represent 'the people' was governing corruptly. Cobbett, in particular, used the phrase 'old corruption' to describe the unreformed political system of the early nineteenth century. 'Old corruption', he said, happily taxed ordinary people

Figure 3 Map of the main industrial areas in Britain in the first half of the eighteenth century

who were engaged in a desperate struggle to make ends meet, in order to pay for its own pleasures and to keep its friends in profitable jobs. In 1815, during an agricultural depression, a new Corn Law was passed through parliament. This prohibited foreign corn from coming into Britain until the domestic price reached 80 shillings (£4) a quarter: a famine price. The effect was to keep the price of bread (the basic food of most working people) artificially high. After 1815, the government was often extremely unpopular. By the late 1820s some members of parliament feared revolution if political change did not come.

Short-term causes

The long-term factors mentioned above help to explain why a people's political movement emerged in the first half of the nineteenth century. They do not, however, explain why Chartism broke out at the particular time it did. To get to grips with this, you need to understand not just the long-term background (vital though that is) but also what historians call 'short-term' causes. To make it easier for you to refer to them separately, these have been numbered below. However, do remember that these factors were inter-linked. When you explain why an important political movement like Chartism erupted, you need to show links between the various factors.

1 The 'Great' Reform Act of 1832

The political system *was* reformed in 1832. A new Whig government, which had come into office in November 1830 under Earl Grey, had persuaded members of parliament that the likely alternative to reform was revolution. The so-called 'Great' Reform Act was the result. But how 'great' was it? The answer to this question is critical to understanding why the People's Charter was drawn up, and why thousands in the late 1830s and early 1840s supported it.

The answer depended on where you were standing. Members of parliament heard the government's proposals for the first time in March 1831; many were appalled. More than one hundred parliamentary constituencies were to be abolished and replaced by new constituencies in the large towns and in the counties where the majority of voters actually lived. There would also be for the first time what was called a 'uniform franchise' in the parliamentary boroughs, where everyone who occupied, or owned, property worth £10 or more according to local rate-books would be entitled to vote. They could not yet calculate it precisely, but members of parliament also knew that a very large number of new voters would be created. As it turned out, the electorate was increased only by about 50% overall, though by a much larger proportion in Scotland, Wales and Ireland, where rights to vote before 1832 had been extremely restricted. Overall, after 1832 about one man in five would be able to vote in a parliamentary election. The majority of the new voters would be small property owners in the so-called middle classes.

Many people *inside* parliament in 1832, then, thought that the 'Great' Reform Act had produced massive, and unwelcome, change. Some even talked excitedly of a 'revolution', even if carried out in a legal way. One prominent anti-reformer, John Wilson Croker, refused to stand for the new parliament because he believed that everything he cared about had been destroyed by his political opponents.

◢ Source 2

The Reform Bill is a stepping stone in England to a republic. The Bill once passed, goodnight to the Monarchy and the Lords and the Church.

John Wilson Croker, 1831 in his **Diaries**, *1857*

Those *outside* parliament tended to see things differently. In particular, many who would shortly be leading Chartists felt betrayed. The hopes of a new parliament which represented a wider range of interests, and which could be relied upon (unlike its predecessor) to pass laws in the interests of the nation as a whole had been dashed. Here is Henry Hetherington (see page 20), the editor of a leading radical magazine, explaining to his readers why he felt bitter, and why he believed his readers should too:

◢ Source 3

... with a little instinctive sense of self-preservation, have the Whigs manufactured a 'great measure'. They knew that the old system could not last, and desiring to establish another as like it as possible, and also to keep their places [to stay in office], they

framed the BILL, in the hope of drawing to the feudal aristocracy and yeomanry of the counties a large reinforcement of the middle class. The Bill was, in effect, an invitation to the shopocrats of the enfranchised towns to join the Whigocrats of the country, and make common cause with them in keeping down the people, and thereby quell the rising spirit of democracy in England.

Henry Hetherington, **Poor Man's Guardian**, 27 October 1832

This, it is true, is a very early reaction to 1832 from an extremely perceptive radical journalist. As the 1830s wore on, and working-class leaders could see what kind of legislation the reformed House of Commons was passing, it became the dominant reaction.

2 Free trade and the 'new political economy'

Early in the nineteenth century, political leaders in Britain were becoming increasingly attracted to new ideas about the running of the economy and society. Most of these ideas derived from a famous book, *Wealth of Nations*, published by the Scottish political economist and philosopher Adam Smith (1726–90) in 1776. It argued that the best way to increase a nation's wealth was to remove all of the tariffs and customs barriers which countries set up and to establish a system of 'free trade'. Free trade would help the consumer, who would benefit from competition between manufacturers and providers of basic services. Other economic and political thinkers developed this line of thinking, notably the so-called 'utilitarians' who took their cue from Jeremy Bentham (1748–1832) in arguing that the prime purpose of government should be to ensure 'the greatest happiness of the greatest number'.

Why should this be a threat to working people? For two reasons. Firstly, the utilitarians believed that, although some modest regulation on behalf of unprotected workers such as women and children was permissible – even desirable – the greater 'happiness' they sought was intimately bound up with the belief that the only proper mechanism for regulating wages, prices and working conditions was market forces in a free-trade economy. Secondly, since the 1820s governments, both Tory and Whig, had increasingly followed free-trade policies. In an expanding economy, such as Britain certainly had during its industrial revolution in the late eighteenth and early nineteenth centuries, free-trade ideas might well help to stimulate innovation and development. These were vital while the population was increasing so rapidly. Between 1801 and 1851, the population of Britain almost doubled – from 8.9 million to 17.9 million – so the creation of new jobs was essential. However, free-trade ideas came at a heavy price for many workers since they involved an attack on old work practices and perceptions of 'rights'. The most obvious of these attacks was the removal of apprenticeship regulations in 1813–14. Apprenticeship had guaranteed the entry to a trade of only appropriately trained workers; it operated as a form of quality control, which gave workers what we might now call a 'formal qualification'. This skill was marketable; apprenticed workers frequently commanded wages more than double those of unskilled labourers. Apprentices served for long periods, however – normally seven years – and the institution of apprenticeship worked against the need of manufacturers for quick recruitment of semi-skilled and unskilled workers able to work in factories and large workshops.

Skilled workers fought bitterly against the repeal of apprenticeship regulations and the wholesale introduction of unskilled labour in many trades. The Luddite disturbances of 1811–16 were similarly motivated by the introduction not of all types of machinery but of those types which did not require skilled operatives. The campaigns had little direct success. Wages in many skilled trades were driven down as workers failed to prevent 'dilution'. They did, however, heighten skilled workers' sense of grievance over what they considered their 'lost rights' and their awareness that collective action was necessary in defence of their position. The campaign continued after 1832, disappointed expectations of parliamentary reform linking political with economic grievances. Just before his death, 'Orator' Hunt put the point powerfully:

◢ Source 4

There are seven millions of men in the United Kingdom, who are rendered so many political outlaws by the Reform Bill: by the provisions of that Act, they are to all intents and purposes so many political slaves. Therefore [we] say, you have deprived us of all share in the making the laws, and we will make laws for ourselves, as far as the regulating the hours of our labour and the amount of our wages. Consequently, one of two things must happen, either the workmen must have more wages and less work, or an equal share in making the laws that are to regulate the measure of labour, wages, and profit.

Henry Hunt, quoted in J. Belchem, **'Orator' Hunt: Henry Hunt and English Working-class Politics** (Oxford University Press, 1985)

Against the consequences of free trade, therefore, workers looked to political change as a means of reasserting ancient rights. Chartism became linked with other strategies, including trade unionism and co-operation, for material betterment. Here are the founders of the Co-Operative Society in the west Yorkshire town of Ripponden asserting in 1832 that workers' rights must be respected because workers were the creators of wealth. This is a statement of what is often called 'the labour theory of value' – meaning that all value ultimately derives from the work which is put into manufacture or the provision of services.

◢ Source 5

1 Labour is the source of all wealth; consequently the working classes have created all the wealth.

2 The working classes, although the producers of wealth, instead of being the richest, are the poorest of the community; hence they cannot be receiving a just recompense [reward] for their labour.

Quoted in D. Thompson (ed), **The Early Chartists** (Macmillan, 1971)

It is interesting to notice that working-class radicals were not alone in their hatred of political economy. They had at least temporary support from those often called Tory humanitarians, a group of landowners and spokesmen for the landed interest who shared sympathy for workers left unprotected by the brutality of the industrial revolution. Few of these people wanted to extend the vote to working people, but they certainly believed that they needed protection against the consequences of free trade. Here is one of the best known of them, Richard Oastler, laying into the Whigs, whom he saw as the natural supporters of the new political economy, in 1832:

◢ **Source 6**

I hate Whig politics with a most perfect hatred ... [they] are the great supporters of the Factory System which is fast destroying the Landed Interest and the Labouring Classes. The time is come when all must join together against the political economists, or this country cannot be saved.

Richard Oastler, quoted in J. T. Ward, **Chartism** (Batsford, 1973)

Chartists were already learning, however, how dangerous 'joining together' could be. Their rhetoric and language would soon stress the importance, not of looking for allies among the privileged, but of uniting the working classes in support of their own political agenda.

3 The New Poor Law

Probably the most important short-term factor explaining why the Chartist movement emerged during the late 1830s was opposition to the Poor Law Amendment Act of 1834, often called the New Poor Law. The new poor law was an extremely controversial measure for many reasons but, as far as working people were concerned, it drew a new, and wildly unfair, distinction between the 'deserving' and the 'undeserving' poor. The new Poor Law Commission aimed to impose more order and central authority on the patchwork system of poor relief which had existed before 1834. In particular, those physically fit 'able-bodied' men who did not find work were to be relieved in workhouses where conditions were deliberately designed to be worse ('less eligible' was the phrase used by the poor law reformers) than those experienced by those who were in work – however low the level of wages paid.

Recent research has confirmed both that most people in need of poor relief continued to receive it in money or other forms of payment outside the workhouse ('outdoor relief') and also that conditions in the workhouse, though basic and sometimes demeaning, were not usually as dreadful as many at the time imagined. This, however, is not the point. The New Poor Law was condemned by Tory humanitarians and radical working-class leaders alike as a callous attack on the rights and dignities of the poor. In an early edition of *Northern Star* (24 February 1838) Bronterre O'Brien condemned the use of state power against working people:

◢ Source 7

The New Poor Act was passed ... to place the whole of the labouring classes at the utter mercy and disposal of the moneyed or property owning classes

> *James Bronterre O'Brien, quoted in M. E. Rose, 'The anti-Poor Law Agitation' in J. T. Ward (ed),* **Popular Movements, 1830–50** *(Macmillan, 1970)*

Samuel Kydd, a young shoemaker in the 1830s, emphasised the crucial link between the new poor law and the loss of rights which was so important to the emergence of Chartism:

◢ Source 8

The passing of the New Poor Law Amendment Act did more to sour the hearts of the labouring population, than did ... all the poverty of the land ... The labourers of England believed that the new poor law was a law to punish poverty; and that the effects of that belief were, to sap the loyalty of the working men, to make them dislike the country of their birth, to brood over their wrongs, to cherish feelings of revenge, and to hate the rich of the land.

> *Samuel Kydd, quoted in D. Thompson,* **The Chartists: Popular Politics in the Industrial Revolution** *(Temple Smith, 1984)*

It was widely noted that both Whigs and Tories supported the Poor Law Amendment Act, enabling working-class leaders to build on their attack that the Reform Act of 1832 was a sham and that enfranchised groups were using their power to pass laws which attacked the interests of working people.

A number of popular disturbances against the introduction of the New Poor Law took place in rural areas in 1835 and 1836, but the most extensive, and best organised, protests took place in the north of England when the Commissioners attempted to bring the new Act to the industrial areas of south Lancashire and west Yorkshire in 1837 and 1838. Monster meetings, attracting more than one hundred thousand people, were held to protest against the Act. In Huddersfield, in June 1837, direct action by several thousands wrecked the workhouse and prevented the election of poor law guardians.

The Commissioners drew back from a full confrontation not only with working people of the industrial areas but with what one assistant commissioner called 'respectable and influential persons' who shared their sense of outrage. Extensive outdoor relief continued and the programme of workhouse building was delayed. However, the damage was done. In west Yorkshire, especially, the mass meetings attacking the new poor law led directly into the support for Chartism as a means of giving back to working people the rights they had lost.

4 The return of economic depression

The first half of the nineteenth century saw many economic crises; the worst of these almost invariably coincided with a revival of radical activity. In the new industrial areas, these usually brought substantial short-term unemployment or short-time working and wage cuts. Those meetings which heralded the beginning of Chartism as a mass movement took place in industrial Lancashire and Yorkshire during the second half of 1838. Reliable statistics about economic performance are difficult to come by but it is clear that the years 1838–42 were among the most difficult of the whole century for working people. In addition to the unemployment crises, bread prices, which had generally been low since the end of the French wars in 1815, started to rise alarmingly. In 1839, wheat reached a peak price of 81 shillings (£4.05) per quarter. The depression of 1842 was one of the most severe in the nineteenth century. About one half of the mechanics and shipbuilders in Dundee were unemployed at this time, for example.

The testimony of ordinary Chartists – often taken when they were defending themselves in trials for conspiracy – puts flesh on the dry bones of statistics. Here is Richard Pilling, a power-loom weaver, charged in 1843 with offences relating to the Plug Plot riots (see pages 6 and 14):

◢ Source 9

After working in the factory seven years, a reduction [of wages] began to creep in one way or the other ... There were some masters always who wanted to give less wages than others. Seeing this to be an evil, and knowing it to be injurious to the master, to the owner of cottage property, and the publican – knowing that all depended on the wages of the working man, I became an opponent to the reduction of wages to the bottom of my soul; and, as long as I live, I shall continue to keep up the wages of labour to the upmost of my power. For taking that part in Stockport, and being the means of preventing many reductions [of wages], the masters combined as one man against me, and neither me nor my children could get a day's employment.

Richard Pilling, quoted in F. C. Mather (ed),
Chartism and Society *(Bell and Hyman, 1980)*

The Methodist minister and people's champion, Reverend Joseph Rayner Stephens, was also well aware of the strong links between economic circumstances and political agitation when he made his famous statement to a mass meeting at Kersal Moor, outside Manchester, on 24 September 1838. He was not implying (as some have suggested) that Chartism was basically an 'economic' movement; rather he believed that Chartism's political programme was necessary if working people were to redress real economic grievances.

◢ Source 10

The principle of the Resolution [to support the People's Charter] ... which he had risen to speak to, was a principle which every man which breathed God's free air and trod God's free earth, to have his home and hearth, and his wife and his children as securely guaranteed to him as of any other man whom the Aristocracy had created ... This question of Universal Suffrage was a knife and fork question after all; this question was a bread and cheese question, notwithstanding all that had been said against it; and if any man asked him what he meant by Universal Suffrage, he would answer, that every working man in the land had a right to have a good coat to his back, a comfortable abode in which to shelter himself and his family, a good dinner upon his table, and no more work than was necessary for keeping him in health, and as much wages for that work as would keep him in plenty.

Reverend Joseph Rayner Stephens, quoted in E. Royle,
Chartism *(Addison Wesley Longman, 1996)*

Two things stand out from the analysis of causes in this chapter. First, the origins of Chartism go back a long way and historians need to understand how long-term factors linked to short-term ones in the 1830s to produce what was to be, by some distance, the largest working-class political movement of the nineteenth century. Second, the causes are both 'political' and 'economic and social'. It is very important to keep this point in mind as you read the later chapters of this book. Chartism was, indeed, a political movement. As you saw in Part One, all of its famous 'Six Points' were political. However, most Chartists supported the People's Charter not because they were believers in some abstract or theoretical notion of a 'well-ordered constitution' founded in male democracy. They wanted the charter because they believed it would bring them material benefits: reduced taxation, fair prices, better wages, improved working conditions and, perhaps most of all, no fears of degrading poverty and 'the workhouse'. Chartism was, then, a political movement but it cannot be properly understood outside the context of its urgent economic and social agenda.

Taking notes

Everyone who is studying for an examination will find it useful to make notes. Notes are a vital revision aid because they help you retain information in manageable form without having to re-read everything you have used in your studies.

What makes good notes?

1 A sensible structure which lets you take down the essential knowledge on a topic.

2 A consistent system of abbreviations which you can understand; no one else needs to! Instead of writing 'Chartism' every time, why not have 'Chrt'? For 'Feargus O'Connor', have 'OCnr'. Remember, though, that Daniel O'Connell was another Irish radical contemporary. Many students mix them up in exam answers, so keep the abbreviated names you use in your notes clearly separate – O'Connell might be 'OCnl'.

3 A good selection of material: leave out all unnecessary words.

4 Proper headings: these will help you to organise and, later, learn your material in an orderly fashion.

---

1 Using the guidance that follows, make your own notes on Chapter One. Most books used for serious study convey information in text which is broken only into paragraphs and chapters; they do not break the text up further into smaller sections with a range of headings, fonts and other design features. When making notes from books like these, you will find it useful to break the material up into headings along the lines employed in this book.

You will find that you are likely to remember material better if you ask yourself *questions* as you select and arrange it. Don't just think 'Why is this relevant?'. Go a bit further. Ask *how* you can use material for particular purposes. This is especially valuable in the case of sources. Examiners are anxious to find out if you can use sources in your answers to questions. Contemporary sources are the raw material from which historians construct their accounts and explanations. They are central to every historical enquiry. The examples below show how you might ask questions of particular material and specific sources.

Use these as a base. You could devise similar questions yourself for other sources. Remember to use this technique when you are tackling the later chapters of this book.

A How far back do demands for parliamentary reform go?

i Read the relevant paragraphs on pages 23–25, noting when before 1832 demands for reform were heard.

ii Read Source 1 (page 24) and note why William Pitt, as prime minister, was so opposed to reform in the 1790s.

B What were the long-term causes of Chartism?

i Go through the bullet points on pages 25–28 which identify some long-term causes. Select key information (especially from the longer sections), remembering to identify some of the places where Chartism later became strong.

ii Study the map in Figure 3 (page 27). Make a list of the areas of Chartist concentration. In your notes, identify these areas (south-west England, north-west England, west Yorkshire, central Scotland, etc.). Examiners are impressed by students who can show some precise geographical awareness when they discuss Chartism.

iii Note which of the 'causes' that you identify are mainly 'political' and which mainly 'economic and social'. You could arrange your notes in two columns to make the differences clearer.

C What were the short-term causes of Chartism?

i Chapter One also identifies four 'short-term' causes (pages 28–36). These concentrate on events or developments in the 1830s. Make a chart showing how each of these causes relates to the long-term factors you have identified.

ii Make subsections for each of these four causes, asking yourself questions as you go through the material. For example, why was apprenticeship important for so many workers? Why was the New Poor Law so hated? You should be able to find at least two reasons for each.

iii Causes often inter-relate. Make a list which shows the links between the various causes being discussed. (Think how opposition to the 'Great' Reform Act (factor 1) might relate to opposition to the New Poor Law (factor 3); think how growing economic depression (factor 4) might suggest to working people that 'free trade' and the 'new political economy' did not necessarily help them.)

iv Make full use of the sources in Chapter One. Begin by understanding what each of the authors is saying. Note the 'political' and the 'economic' reasons for discontent which are made; put them in separate columns, referring precisely in each case to the author and type (speech, newspaper article, resolution at a meeting, etc.) of the source, so that you can make precise references in your essays and exam answers. Relate your understanding to material in more than one source. For example, what evidence in the Chartist Land Co-Operative Society resolution (Source 5, page 32) is supported by Henry Hunt in Source 4, page 31? How would you select material from Source 9, page 35 and Source 10, page 36 to demonstrate the importance of social and economic causes in Chartism?

2 Having read, and made notes on, the material in Chapter One, which of the various long-term and short-term factors are *most* important in explaining why Chartism emerged as a mass movement in 1838? In your notes, explain briefly why you think some factors are more important than others. In almost all history tasks, you will be asked to say on the basis of what evidence you have reached a particular opinion.

CHAPTER TWO

WHO SUPPORTED THE CHARTISTS?

Objectives

⊿ To analyse the nature of support for Chartism among different groups

⊿ To appreciate that, although Chartism was predominantly a movement supported by working people, those working people came from different backgrounds and were in different circumstances

⊿ To examine the importance of religion for many Chartists.

We know a great deal about the Chartist leaders and a great deal, too, about their ideas. Because they appear in so much of the literature as little more than 'faces in the crowd', however, we know far less about those who supported the movement. A lot of what we *do* know comes from the evidence of the leaders, so we have to treat it with caution. After all, they spent so much time 'on the road' that they could hardly develop an intimate knowledge of the locations they visited. Feargus O'Connor boasted in *Northern Star* that he had given speeches at 22 large public meetings in 11 different towns and cities as far apart as Bristol and Edinburgh in the month between 18 December 1838 and 15 January 1839 alone.

In this chapter we try to understand the nature and extent of support for Chartism. We examine middle-class support, which was not inconsiderable in Chartism's early years, in Chapter Four. Here we concentrate on support for the Chartists among working people. A range of sources is available, not least the evidence of *local* Chartist leaders. They, too, were active in taking the message out to lecture and assembly halls and, where necessary, into the public houses. Figure 4 shows the programme of William Bairstow as he travelled through Lancashire and south Yorkshire in January 1841. We know from local research that Bairstow's lecture in the Owenite Hall of Science on 14 January 1841 drew 1 500 people.

Figure 5 shows a complete plan of weekly lectures to be given by seventeen local lecturers (none of them well known) in the first three

3rd to 28th January 1841	
3rd	Manchester
4th	Newton Heath
5th	Sheffield
6th	Sheffield
7th	Staleybridge
8th	Stockport
10th	Newton Heath and Failsworth
11th	Hunsworth and Bolton
12th	Preston
13th	Wigan
14th	Liverpool
15th	Warrington
18th	Warrington
19th	Ashton
20th	Manchester
21st	Salford
22nd	Radcliffe Bridge
24th	Rochdale
25th	Oldham
26th	Droylsden
27th	Middleton
28th	Mottram

Figure 4 William Bairstow's programme as he travelled through Lancashire and south Yorkshire in January 1841
Source: D. Jones, *Chartism and the Chartists* (St Martin's Press, 1975), p103

months of 1841 in 12 separate venues in and around Manchester. Virtually all of the slots are filled in and it is clear that Manchester, Salford, Oldham and Rochdale were fertile ground in which the Chartist message could be spread at that time.

It is clear that, in the peak years at least, Chartism was indeed a national movement. Within this, however, certain trends in support have long been recognised:

◢ it was much stronger in urban areas than in rural ones
◢ it was especially strong in the new industrial districts

PLACES	Time of Meeting	January					February				March			
		3	10	17	24	31	7	14	21	28	7	14	21	28
Tib-street, Manchester. Sunday	6	8	2	5	13	14	3	6	5	4	2	12	3	9
Brown-street Do.	6	6	3	9	8	11	17	2	7	5	6	10	14	4
Salford Do.	6½	2	7	17	10	6	8	3	9	2	4	5	6	11
Oldham, Do.	2	13	11	2	14	3	13	14	11	6	5	2	13	14
Do. Do.	6	12	14	2	11	3	12	11	13	6	5	2	12	15
Middleton, Do.	6	9	17	3	6	4	8	5	4	7	3	9	8	10
Ashton, Do.	2½	3	8	10	7	6	10	4	13	8	9	4	7	3
Newton Heath Do.	2½		1				6				8			
Do. Saturday	7					4			7				6	
Bolton, Monday Evening	8	16	15	16	2	15	16	11	15	16	15	16	2	16
Mottram, Thursday Evening	8				3				2			11		
Droylsden, Tuesday	8	3	5	2	6	7	3	8	10	11	4	9	3	2
Failsworth, Sunday	6		1		9		17		14		10		5	
Rochdale, Do.	2	14	5	11	3	2	12	11	17	9	14	3	16	6
Do. Do.	6	14	5	11	3	2	12	11	17	9	14	3	16	6

LECTURERS
1. James Leech, Manchester
2. William Tillman, Do.
3. Charles Conner, Do.
4. Joseph Linney, Do.
5. Edward Curran, Do.
6. James Cartledge, Do.
7. William Shearer, Do.
8. John Campbell, Salford
9. William Bell, Do.
10. Richard Littler, Do.
11. James Greaves, Austerlands
12. John Greaves, Shaw
13. Francis Lowes, Oldham
14. Henry Smethurst, Do.
15. Richard Marsden, Bolton
16. John Gardiner, Do.
17. Edward Clark, Manchester

Figure 5 A complete plan of weekly lectures to be given in and around Manchester during the first three months of 1841

Source: E. Evans, *The Birth of Modern Britain, 1780–1914* (Addison Wesley Longman, 1997)

◢ it tended not to be strong among unskilled workers and casual labourers

◢ it was less strong in London, at least in the early stages, than in many other urban areas. London had always been the acknowledged capital of radical politics; both leadership of, and support for, Chartism proved stronger and more tenacious elsewhere in 1838–39. The capital did, however, become more significant from 1841 onwards

◢ it tended to be strong wherever large numbers of craftsmen congregated, particularly if those crafts had been threatened by mechanisation or by the influx of unskilled and semi-skilled workers.

Recent work in the localities has made it possible to produce a more rounded picture of support. The general trend of this work has been to demonstrate that certain places, although not hotbeds of radicalism, had more Chartist activity than was once thought.

Case study: Liverpool

◢ Source 1

[In Liverpool] the regular meetings continued to be well supported throughout 1841, besides a number of larger meetings and other activities. In April, Peter McDouall [a qualified surgeon from Ashton-under-Lyne, Cheshire, and celebrated Chartist lecturer] spoke in the Association Room in Preston Street to between 850 and 900 people, hundreds being turned away due to lack of space ... A discussion class was formed in May, and met every Sunday evening ... In August, Lawrence Pitkeithly reported to the [Northern] Star on the Liverpool Committee which organised the despatch and distribution of that newspaper and other literature to Ireland.

K. Moore, 'Liverpool in the Chartist era' in J. Belchem (ed), **Popular Politics, Riot and Labour: Essays in Liverpool History** (Liverpool University Press, 1992)

Moore acknowledged that support for Chartism was stronger further east in Lancashire. Nevertheless it followed a similar pattern in 1841 to that of the movement elsewhere. The committee which ran Chartism in the city was dominated by skilled male workers. Of the members identified by occupation and reported to the National Charter Association, eight were tailors and four were shoemakers – well known as 'radical trades'. Only one of the 26 members of the committee, a porter, seems not to have been skilled. Chartism got going later than in Manchester, however, and largely in outraged response to the sentence passed on John Frost (see page 13). Following the strikes in 1842 it collapsed more abjectly than in most other places. Moore offered a number of reasons to explain Liverpool's relatively limited support:

1 Liverpool had a larger proportion of completely unskilled workers in 1841 (about 25%) than Manchester or Salford (10%).

2 The introduction of the new poor law in the late 1830s caused less offence in Liverpool than elsewhere since harsh local regulations had been in place since 1821.

3 Liverpool had the nation's largest proportion of Irish-born in its population (more than 22% according to the census of 1851). This contributed to the overall proportion of low-skilled workers there. However, a more powerful reason was that almost all the Irish immigrants were Catholics. Since they were frequently accused of taking the jobs of native-born workers, or of driving down wages, the potential for harmony within the workforce was considerably less. 'No Popery', indeed, was a frequent cry as religious disharmony between Protestants and Catholics became an increasingly important part of Liverpool politics.

4 New ideas on 'free trade' (see pages 30–33) proved much more popular among skilled workers in Liverpool than in most other British towns. Liverpool was, of course, the country's leading port for trade with the Americas and the opportunities for trade expansion were seen as bringing fresh opportunities and new prosperity for the skilled workers in the docks and commercial areas of the city. Whereas opposition to free trade was a powerful route into Chartism elsewhere, it was not so in Liverpool.

5 Liverpool afforded fewer opportunities for women to do paid work than most other cities.

We can, of course, use this list to confirm what *were* the circumstances which helped bring about support for Chartism in the industrial areas:

◢ the presence of a large number of skilled workers well used to political discussion and organisation but now under threat

◢ fear of the new poor law. In some places, this was extended into more general opposition to an oppressive and hostile state passing laws which harmed the interests of the lower orders

◢ a sense of ancient rights being threatened by alien ideas such as free trade and the new political economy (see Chapter 1)

◢ a growing sense of helplessness and vulnerability in the face of adverse economic circumstances. As we saw in Chapter One, the late 1830s and 1840s were periods of violent economic fluctuation and uncertainty.

The role of women

As we saw in Part One the charter aimed to secure universal *manhood* suffrage. Yet work during the 1980s and 1990s has demonstrated the important role which women played in supporting Chartism. Few national Chartist leaders actively campaigned for women to have the vote, although an early draft of the Chartist Petition in 1837 included universal suffrage, for which Lovett later claimed credit. The two prominent Chartists who did, the London journalist John Watkins, in *Address to the Women of England*, and the Manchester carpenter and trade union activist Reginald J. Richardson, would have restricted it to unmarried women and widows. As Watkins put it: 'not wives – for they and their husbands are one, or ought to be'. Richardson's pamphlet *The Rights of Woman* was written while he was in Lancaster gaol in 1840:

◢ Source 2

I have ... shown you that woman bears her share in the burdens of state, and contributes more than her fair proportion to the wealth of the country. I ask you, is there a man, knowing these things, who can lay his hand upon his heart, and say, Women ought not to interfere in political affairs? No: I hope there is none for the honour of my sex ...

I think, nay I believe, that God ordained woman 'to temper man'. I believe from this reason, that she ought to share in the making of laws for the government of the commonwealth, in the same manner as she would join with her husband in the councils of his household.

Reginald J. Richardson, quoted in D. Thompson (ed),
The Early Chartists (Macmillan, 1971)

By no means all women involved with Chartism accepted Richardson's analysis. Some were concerned that 'votes for women' might be taken up in order to strengthen property owners and thus weaken the working classes still further. Others were concerned to safeguard what they saw as their primary role as household managers and mothers. This was the line taken by the Female Political Union of Newcastle-upon-Tyne, as reported in *Northern Star* in February 1839:

◢ Source 3

We have been told that the province of woman is her home, and that the field of politics should be left to men; this we deny; the nature of things renders it impossible, and the conduct of those who give advice is at variance with the principles they assert. Is it not true that the interests of our fathers, husbands, and brothers, ought to be ours? If they are oppressed and impoverished, do we not share those evils with them? If so, ought we not to resent the infliction of those wrongs upon them? We have read the records of the past, and our hearts have responded to the historian's praise of those women, who struggled against tyranny and urged their countrymen to be free or die …

We have seen that because the husband's earnings could not support his family, the wife has been compelled to leave her home neglected and, with her infant children, work at soul and body degrading toil …

We have searched and found that the cause of these evils is the Government of the country being in the hands of a few of the upper and middle classes, while the working men who form the millions, the strength and wealth of the country, are left without the Pale of the Constitution, their wishes never consulted, and their interests sacrificed by the ruling factions, who have created useless officers and enormous salaries for their own aggrandisement [enrichment] …

Northern Star, *February 1839, quoted in D. Thompson (ed),*
***The Early Chartists** (Macmillan, 1971)*

This perspective is, perhaps, understandable coming from the north-east of England, where the main sources of employment were the mines, the docks and engineering – predominantly male preserves, with women in a purely supportive capacity. The view of the Newcastle women also closely matches that of artisan radicalism, with its hatred of 'old corruption' (see page 10). In the textile areas, things were different. Textile production depended on the work of women and children at least as much as on that of men. Much of Richardson's pamphlet, indeed, was given up to demonstrating the extensive employment of women in the new manufacturing areas.

The importance of women in the Chartist movement, at least until 1842, has been under-estimated partly because, as Dorothy Thompson scornfully notes:

◢ Source 4

The early historians, from Gammage to the Fabians, were concerned to present Chartism as a serious political movement. They played down all aspects, such as social occasions, tea parties, Sunday Schools, processions and other picturesque or ritualistic elements which belonged to an older tradition, contrasting them unfavourably with the rational and modernising aspects of the movement. In the same way, most contemporary observers ... saw the irrational and the decorative, in which they mostly included the female, parts of the movement as lessening and demeaning it.

D. Thompson, ***The Chartists: Popular Politics in the Industrial Revolution*** *(Temple Smith, 1984)*

It is extremely difficult to get anything other than the most general picture of the importance of women in the Chartist movement because so few women aspired to be local leaders. Also, the authorities usually avoided arresting women radicals, probably to avoid adverse publicity or charges of victimisation, so legal records yield very little information about them. A few, like Susanna Inge from London and Marguerite Milburn from Crook (County Durham), established national reputations as lecturers during the 1840s. Miss E. J. Miles was President of the City of London Female Chartist association. Far more are lost to the historical record, though they may have numbered up to a quarter of the total Chartist support in the 1840s. Certainly, at least a hundred separate female radical associations are known to have existed, quite apart from women's contribution to local branches of the National Charter Association.

More is known about why women came into the movement and the kind of work they did. The following were important:

1 the operation of the new poor law and fear of the workhouse. This seemed particularly threatening to women. A meeting of The Female Inhabitants of Elland (near Leeds) passed a resolution proposed by one Mrs Grasby:

◢ Source 5

... this Meeting considers the new Poor Law Amendment Act an infringement on our rights. Because it considers it to be unmercifully oppressive and tyrannical, sparing neither sex nor age ... Women have still more to do with this cruel measure

than men. *Their feelings were more susceptible and the pangs of being separated from those to whom they had been used to look for support, and from the children of their own bearing were more severe ... than it was possible for men to feel (cheers). They ought also to resist it from a sense of duty. It was their duty to be, each one, a helpmate to her husband – to soothe his sorrows, but this law prevented her from being able to do so.*

*Reported in **Northern Star**, 17 February 1838*

2 raising funds for the defence of Chartists accused of crimes and for the families of those transported

3 organisation of social activities designed to keep groups together and also for fund-raising. These included processions, railway excursions, tea parties and musical festivals

4 teetotal and temperance societies. Women were particularly vulnerable to menfolk who drank away a substantial portion of the weekly wages in the public house or beershop on the day they were paid. Abstaining from drink was also, for many radicals and Chartists, a way of demonstrating their seriousness and 'respectability'

5 running Sunday schools and Bible classes

6 organising family budgets to favour those who supported the People's Charter and seeking to avoid shopkeepers and other suppliers known to be hostile to the cause. This strategy was called 'Exclusive Dealing'.

◢ Source 6

The female radicals of the Bradford district, amounting to upward of 600, walked in procession through the principal streets headed by a band of music and banners ... at the head of the procession there was carried by a woman a large printed board with the words 'exclusive dealing'.

Northern Star, *August 1839, quoted in D. Thompson, **The Chartists: Popular Politics in the Industrial Revolution** (Temple Smith, 1984)*

Chartists and trade unions

Recent detailed studies have challenged some old assumptions here also. It is now clear that, in certain areas of industrial Britain, relations between Chartism and trade unionism were close – at least until after the strikes of 1842. Older ideas of a stand-off between skilled workers who valued their ability to bargain with employers for high wages and good conditions on the one hand and less fortunate workers who embraced the People's Charter as a 'desperation' strategy when times were hard have been largely exploded. It is true that many of the best-paid and most secure workers and those with skills which were in demand during the early industrial revolution – stonemasons and engineers stand out – could see little advantage in joining a Chartist organisation. Firstly, some risked dismissal for allying with dangerous or subversive political movements. Secondly, some skilled workers saw genuine benefit to themselves in supporting free trade; they thus challenged the assumptions underpinning radical ideas in the late 1830s and early 1840s (see pages 30–33).

Most trade unionists were not in such a secure or privileged position in the workplace, however. For them, association with Chartism was a sensible strategy in times of economic distress or attack by employers. It is clear that many cotton spinners in Glasgow were encouraged into Chartism by the prosecutions which followed their strike in 1837, events which increased their sense of alienation from government and from employers clearly hostile to unionism. In Manchester in 1838, the Trades Council, representing a wide range of skilled workers, participated in the Kersal Moor meeting and also boycotted celebrations to mark the coronation of Queen Victoria. The language of their protest recalls that of popular radical attacks on excessive government corruption, though with clear evidence of class antagonism:

◢ Source 7

We, the Trades Unions have had no encouragement from our national and local rulers to join in any of their schemes, since we find the wealthy, in and out of parliament, conspiring against the labouring poor to deprive them of the rights of industry, and withholding from them the political rights and liberties of free-born British subjects … The forthcoming Coronation will convince the government that the people are becoming tired of the system which encourages luxurious idleness, excessive taxation, constant persecutions of the poor, and the useless squanderings of the hard earnings of the labouring millions.

Manchester and Salford Advertiser, 30 June 1838, quoted in R. A. Sykes, 'Early Chartism and trade unionism' in J. Epstein and D. Thompson (eds), **The Chartist Experience: Studies in Working-class Radicalism and Culture** (Macmillan, 1982)

Similarly, it was the leaders of the engineering workers in Manchester who called for the strikes in August 1842 as a means of obtaining not only wage increases but also the People's Charter. By this time, according to Sykes, years of 'Chartist enthusiasm' in south Lancashire had made trade unionists much keener on combined action: 'The connections were there in shared ideas, personnel, leaders, newspapers and not infrequently expressions of support for Chartism by unions acting as unions'.

We should not assume that what held for Manchester, the centre of the most advanced industrial area on earth in the early 1840s, held good for the whole of Britain. In north Staffordshire, where colliers were involved in a bitter strike in the summer of 1842, the miners stated publicly: 'We have nothing to do with any Political question; our dispute is simply upon the price of labour.' By mid-August, however, the situation had changed. Thomas Cooper (see pages 18–19) and the Potteries shoemaker and local activist John Richards were speaking from the same public platform as the colliers and proposing the motion 'that all labour cease until the People's Charter becomes the law of the land' (Robert Fyson, 'The Crisis of 1842', in J. Epstein and D. Thompson (eds), *The Chartist Experience* (Macmillan, 1982) p207). It is clear that, in the most heavily industrial areas of England (south Lancashire, west Yorkshire and north Staffordshire), links between Chartism and trade unionism were both close and intended to be mutually supporting, at least until the collapse of the strikes in the late summer of 1842. In the north-east, too, representatives of the Miners' Association, William Dixon and William Grocott, were strong Chartist sympathisers. Ever alert to opportunity, O'Connor extended the title of his newspaper to *The Northern Star and National Trades Journal* in 1842. He urged his supporters:

◢ **Source 8**

… keep your eye fixed upon the great Trades' Movement now manifesting itself throughout the country, and I would implore you to act by all other trades as you have acted by the Colliers. Attend their meetings and give them your sympathy; but upon no account interpose the Charter as an obstacle to their proceedings. All labour and labourers must unite; and they will speedily discover that the Charter is the only standard under which they can successfully rally.

*Quoted in J. T. Ward, **Chartism** (Batsford, 1973)*

The Chartists continually proclaimed their message that the People's Charter was the only way to ensure workers' social rights. It was difficult to make such a message stick, however, in time of good trade and strong bargaining positions. Many skilled workers thought that getting higher wages from an employer desperate to increase productivity during a trade boom was an easier task than pressing on them what many considered a revolutionary programme of democratic reform. Thus, Chartists had to tread carefully. O'Connor gave ample space in *Northern Star* to messages designed to convince both trade unionists and members of other organisations supported by working men that only a radical change in the structure of political power (by adopting the People's Charter) would serve to improve their circumstances. He knew, however, that many would reject the lesson.

The relationship between Chartism and trade unionism is, therefore, complex. Two interesting observations conclude this section. Both suggest that Chartism had a permanent influence on trade union leaders:

1 Within three years of the collapse of the strikes of 1842, leading unions had established a national organisation for the first time. These included the miners, potters and typographers (printers). The national organisation of the Chartists was probably both a model and a spur.

2 When the so-called 'new-model' unions became established during the 1850s, their leaders were among the strongest supporters of further parliamentary reform. Two of them, William Newton and William Allan, attended the last Chartist National Convention in 1858.

Chartism and religion

When he addressed a meeting of the Ipswich (Suffolk) Working Men's Association in February 1838, the local wine merchant Nathaniel Whimper stated that the association should support democracy because equal political and social rights were an essential part of the Christian message. His reaction was a very common one. The Glasgow Universal Suffrage Association showed its contempt for local clergymen who refused to support the People's Charter by organising alternative Sunday services addressed by Chartist preachers.

The great majority of Chartists, it is certain, were believers, although they frequently faced criticism which suggested that they were all Godless:

◢ Source 9

[Supporters of Chartism are] Republicans, Infidels, Sabbath-breakers and Blasphemers who are, unhappily, a curse to themselves, and a curse to the land that owns them.

'C. L.', **The Real Chartist** *(London, 1848)*

This criticism echoed the convenient attack on the artisan radicals of the 1790s that they were 'Jacobins [supporters of the extreme wing of French revolutionaries] and atheists'. Chartism did attract a number of 'free-thinkers', but they were dwarfed by those who acknowledged clear religious allegiance. Of 73 Chartist prisoners questioned about this in 1840 and 1841, 26 (the largest number) said that they were Church of England and 15 said they were Methodists of varying kinds; only nine said that they had no religion. When the leader of the Leicester framework knitters, a man called Finn, introduced a resolution to establish the Leicester and Leicestershire Political Union, he described the Church of England as an 'incubus [an oppressive burden] upon the people' but was careful to reassure the meeting that he was not an 'infidel' [unbeliever]. Two extremely well-known Chartists, Joseph Rayner Stephens and William Hill, editor of *Northern Star* from 1837 to 1843, were ordained ministers, albeit highly unusual ones. Dr Arthur Wade, Church of England Vicar of Warwick, like Stephens, was a member of the first Chartist National Convention in 1839; he also marched at the head of a trade union procession.

A number of Chartists, however, wished the movement to cleanse religion of unhelpful, even Christian, associations. The Church of England was singled out for particular attack, partly because of its long tradition of opposition to any kind of reform.

◢ Source 10

I am delighted with what you state in your reference to the progress of Chartist Christianity ... against the long-faced hypocritical pharisees [name given to a self-righteous person, after a strict Jewish order] of the day, whose religion consists in making long prayers, devouring widows' houses and dutiful submission to the 'powers that be' which powers, they would ... make us believe, are 'ordained by God' ... By all means get rid of the 'black slugs'; by all means protect the consciences and the cabbages of the poor from the 'black slugs'.

Letter from the Birmingham Chartist Arthur O'Neill, 1841, quoted in D. Thompson, **The Chartists: Popular Politics in the Industrial Revolution** (Temple Smith, 1984)

Bronterre O'Brien was characteristically more extreme:

◢ Source 11

You uniformly prostitute religion to the maintenance of civil tyranny. [The people] see that holy writ [the Bible] abounds from one end of the volume to the other in denunciation against usury and tyranny, and in threats of divine vengeance against oppressors of all kinds, and yet in the teeth of these denunciations and solemn menaces, they behold you employing all the power of your craft to bolster up the system.

Open letter to clergy of the Established Church, published in McDouall's Chartist and Republican Journal, quoted in H. U. Faulkner, **Chartism and the Churches** (London, 1916)

In some districts, Chartists established their own churches. Arthur O'Neill was minister of one in Birmingham; others were founded in central Scotland and in the west of England. Scotland, in particular, became the unofficial centre of 'Christian Chartism', its message steadily plugged in *Chartist Circular*, a journal which sold more than twenty thousand copies a week at the end of the 1830s:

◢ Source 11

Christian Chartists! Ye have now begun to worship God in your own churches. Go on and prosper, and the Almighty will bless you ... Let us march triumphantly forward on the sacred way that leads to civil and religious liberty, equality and happiness. Let us press forward to the glorious goal of Universal Suffrage, until we reach it; and let Christian Chartism be (what it ought to be) a deep, religious, political feeling, implanted in our minds, by the Eternal, fostered by education, and perfected by circumstances, having benevolence and honesty for its practice, and the happiness of man for its object.

Chartist Circular, *29 August 1840, quoted in E. Royle,* **Chartism**
(Addison Wesley Longman, 1996)

◢ Source 12

In every district there ought to be a Chartist Church planted for the benefit of Chartist families. It may be a private house, a school, or a public hall, tended by an association, for public meetings, education and religious worship; and every Sabbath day a gospel should be preached in it by a religious, honest missionary, chosen by the Chartists.

Chartist Circular, *28 March 1840, quoted in P. Hollis (ed),*
Class and Conflict in Nineteenth-century England, 1815–50 *(Routledge, 1973)*

This initiative can be seen almost as a kind of exclusive dealing (see page 49) but in churches rather than in produce. The position on which most Chartists could agree was that:

◢ no church should enjoy any special privileges

◢ the legal privileges given to the Church of England, whose hierarchy was notably anti-reformist, were particularly unacceptable.

Thus when the Chartist National Convention passed a resolution on religion in 1851 it advocated a complete separation of the Church of England and the state and the enforced transfer of all church property to the state.

Chartism was, therefore, ***anti-clerical***; very few Chartists were anti-Christian.

KEY TERM

Anti-clericalism – opposition to the influence, or rule, of the clergy. Anti-clericalism was an important element in radicalism from the late eighteenth century onwards. In Britain, it tended to be concentrated in particular on opposition to the Church of England, both because the Church of England was the state, 'official' church and because church leaders generally opposed all reform. During the Chartist period, anti-clericalism may be seen as a key element of continuity within an existing radical tradition.

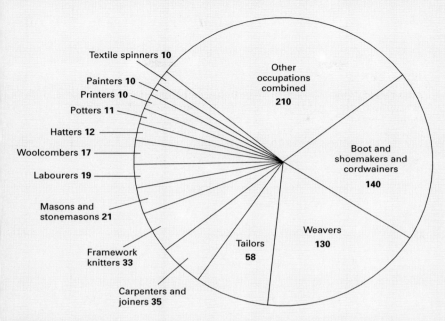

Figure 6 Leading occupations of Chartists nominated to the General Council, printed in *Northern Star*, 1841
Source: D. Jones, *Chartism and the Chartists* (Allen Lane, 1975), pp30–32

Useful information can often be gained from looking at historical data in the form of graphs, maps and charts. Figures 6 and 7 present information about the social composition of Chartism and its regional strength. Look at them carefully and then answer the following questions:

1 On the evidence of the pie-chart in Figure 6, what types of worker seem to have been attracted to Chartism?

2 On the evidence of the map in Figure 7, where does Chartism appear to have been strongest in 1848, and where weakest?

3 How far does the evidence in this chapter support the conclusions you have reached in your answers to questions 1 and 2?

4 What kinds of historical questions can maps, charts and diagrams help you answer?

5 What reservations might you have in using Figures 6 and 7 as evidence about support for Chartism?

Figure 7 Locations of delegates to the Chartist National Convention of 1848
Source: Compiled from information given in R. G. Gammage, *History of the Chartist Movement, 1837–54* (1894; Merlin Press, 1969), p301

TASKS

Clue to answering Question 3: Not all of the information in this chapter will be relevant, but it is useful for you to get used to *selecting* what you need from often much longer pieces of evidence. The skill of relevant selection is the key to much progress in historical understanding at this level.

Clue to answering Question 4: Begin by looking at *this* evidence, and notice how the information is arranged. Then, perhaps in discussion with others in your group, make a list of other historical questions or issues for which maps, charts and diagrams could be useful.

Clue to answering Question 5: When answering questions like this, you need to have a checklist in mind. Among the questions you might ask are the following:

a Are these sources about change or are they 'snapshots' of the situation at a particular time?

b Are their authors likely to be reliable? When was the evidence collected?

c What can I learn about ordinary Chartist membership from evidence about those nominated to be leaders, or to represent ordinary Chartists?

d Is there likely to be a clear relationship between the places from which delegates were nominated and places where Chartism was strong? Should I be cross-checking this evidence with other information?

CHAPTER THREE

HOW EFFECTIVE WAS CHARTIST LEADERSHIP?

Objectives

⊿ To understand the importance of leadership to the Chartist movement

⊿ To examine the ideas of leading Chartists

⊿ To analyse the role of a leading individual, Feargus O'Connor

⊿ To evaluate and interpret primary source material by understanding and extracting information from it and then reaching conclusions about Chartist leadership.

Leadership was crucial to the Chartists. Most of its supporters were not well educated; many suffered acute economic distress and lived in conditions which gave little opportunity for quiet reflection. They looked to their leaders to provide them not only with inspiring speeches but also to show an understanding of their needs and aspirations, as well as contributing to the wider culture of working people. Until fairly recently, the quality of Chartist leadership was not rated highly. When essay questions were set which asked 'Why was Chartism so much less successful than the Anti-Corn Law League?', examiners expected division and weak leadership to figure prominently among the explanations offered.

If leaders were not divided by tactics and ideas, then they were by vanity and contending egos. Mark Hovell, whose important book is considered in Chapter Five, thought that both faults fatally undermined the movement:

⊿ Source 1

*Very soon [*in the autumn of 1838*] the breach between the preachers of violence and the preachers of peaceful agitation was already complete and a campaign of denunciation had begun. O'Connor scoffed at the 'moral philosophers'. Stephens denounced the Birmingham leaders as 'old women', whilst younger and more reckless leaders, like Harney, who was to represent Newcastle-upon-Tyne [*at the forthcoming Chartist National Convention] loudly proclaimed their lack of confidence in such things as Conventions. The crisis came in early December. The Edinburgh Chartists had passed a series of resolutions condemning violent language and repudiating physical* force. These 'moral-force' resolutions called forth a torrent of denunciation from O'Connor, Harney, Dr John Taylor, and others. A furious controversy followed. Various Chartist bodies threatened to go to pieces on the question ...

How exaggerated a notion some of the delegates [at the Chartist National Convention in February 1839] had of their own importance appears from the motion, passed on the 13th on the proposition of O'Brien, that the House of Commons be invited to meet the Convention at the Crown and Anchor Tavern on the 27th of February to disabuse the minds of the members of that House as to the character and intentions of the Convention. Delegates wore 'M.C.' after their names after the fashion of 'M.P.'. They imagined that they had sufficient influence to meet the House of Commons on equal if not superior terms. They repeatedly argued that they had been elected by a much greater number of voters than those who sent men to Westminster, consequently they were entitled to at least as great a share of power as Parliament.

M. Hovell, **The Chartist Movement** (1918; Manchester University Press, 1970)

Was Hovell's harsh judgement justified, or have historians since presented a more sophisticated, as well as a more sympathetic, understanding of the nature of Chartist leadership and the problems it faced? In this chapter, you have the opportunity to enquire into Chartist leadership, using the evidence provided by many of those leaders themselves.

This chapter first considers some of the main divisions within the movement and then moves on to look at the strengths which Chartist leaders showed. It presents a case study of O'Connor's leadership and also poses a basic, but frequently overlooked, question: 'Given the circumstances of the time and the weapons available to them, what did constitute effective leadership?'

Physical and moral force

Many historians used to think that Chartist leaders failed to match up to the task of leadership. All too quickly they split over tactics; misleadingly, historians used to divide Chartists into 'physical-force' and 'moral-force' men and built up a picture almost of two armed camps. It is true that a basic division existed between those who believed that moral pressure should be brought on the authorities to grant the

People's Charter and those who put much more faith in direct action – including violence. It is also true that 'moral-force' arguments were much more likely to be found in the mouths of those who came from the educated and more established tradition of artisan radicalism. The London Working Man's Association (see Part 1) is a prime example of a 'moral-force' organisation. By contrast, when George Julian Harney formed the London Democratic Association in March 1838, intending it to be a much more 'popular' organisation which supported O'Connor and made use of the rhetoric of violence, he is said to have created a 'physical-force' counterpart to the LWMA.

The following two statements also seem to emphasise the distinction:

◢ Source 2

Remember PEACE, LAW, ORDER, LOYALTY AND UNION, these are our Mottoes – under these banners we will gather the strength of the people – under these banners the people possess a giant's strength; but if they abandon them, they become but an infant in a giant's hand.

Thomas Attwood, accepting an invitation to address a meeting on Glasgow Green, 5 May 1838, quoted in J. T. Ward, **Chartism** *(Batsford, 1970)*

◢ Source 3

They had had a slight taste of physical force in the north. A short time since some of the metropolitan police were sent down to Dewsbury, but the boys of that noble town sent them home again. His desire was to try moral force as long as possible, even to the fullest extent, but he would always have them bear in mind, that it is better to die freemen than to live slaves. Every conquest which was called honourable had been achieved by physical force ... He hoped and trusted that out of the exercise of that judgement which belonged exclusively to the working class, a union would arise, and from that union a moral power would be created, sufficient to establish the rights of the poor man; but if this failed, then let every man raise his arm in defence of that which his judgement told him was justice.

Feargus O'Connor, speech at Westminster Palace Yard, 17 September 1838, quoted in R. G. Gammage, **History of the Chartist Movement,1837–54** *(1894; Merlin Press, 1969)*

We should, however, be cautious about what seems an obvious distinction. It is worth remembering the following points:

1 Many Chartists used the language of violence as the natural accompaniment of a speech. O'Connor was only one of many to find that it got a good response at public meetings. It would be rash to assume that physical-force rhetoric actually meant urging people to rebel. Time and again, Chartist leaders talked the language of resistance (which at the very least implied violence) without ever intending to lead rebellion. On the rare occasions when armed resistance was tried, as at Newport (Monmouthshire) in November 1839 or in Sheffield and Bradford in January 1840 (see Chronology of important events, page 6), it was easily put down. Chartist leaders knew that a failed rising was the worst outcome.

2 Some leaders who would be considered obvious 'moral-force' men actually used the language of violence. Robert Lowery, who became the leader of 'temperance Chartism' from 1842, told a magistrate in April 1839:

◢ Source 4

I have a pike at home ... all our people should have pikes and arms ... All should have guns, for the man that could shoot a Pheasant would shoot a Tyrant – we will have our rights.

Robert Lowery, quoted in D. Thompson (ed), **The Early Chartists** *(Macmillan, 1971)*

The journalist and hero of 'the war of the unstamped', Henry Hetherington (see Part 1), explained why at least the language of physical force was necessary:

◢ Source 5

The manner in which physical force had been discussed by some of their members had been the cause of a great many persons not taking an active part in the proceedings, and the use of such language had been a handle to their enemies ... In his late mission, he found that the middle classes invariably raised objections against them in consequence of this constant recurrence to physical force ... He would, when he found the people had tried the influence of moral force, and had

found it insufficient to answer them, be found doing his duty as one of the foremost
of the physical-force men.

> **Henry Hetherington,** Northern Star, *27 April 1839, quoted in P. Hollis (ed),*
> **Class and Conflict in Nineteenth-century England, 1815–50** *(Routledge, 1973)*

Physical-force language, then, is to be found on the lips of moderate
reformers. It can be seen as a device, or a strategy, rather than as a
clear call to arms.

3 The rhetoric of physical force was also probably necessary once the
Chartist National Convention of 1839 revealed the wide variety of
opinions and the obvious dangers of disunity. Most leaders of the
National Charter Association relied on it in the 1840s as a means of
trying to establish unity among working people. It also put clear
water between the different approaches of the Complete Suffrage
Movement of Joseph Sturge (see Chronology of important events,
page 6) on the one hand and the 'new move' of education Chartism
embraced by William Lovett and Harry Collins on the other.
Physical-force rhetoric became a useful weapon in asserting class
solidarity against middle-class 'traitors' and the wiles of the Anti-
Corn Law League. This is a reason why the approach appealed to a
certain type of historian anxious to assert that Chartism was the
first expression of British working-class consciousness. How much
physical-force rhetoric actually *achieved* is another matter. The
distinction between promise and performance on violence agonised
most of the leading Chartists at one time or another and certainly
two of the most thoughtful: James Bronterre O'Brien and George
Julian Harney (see pages 19 and 22).

Division

It is futile to deny that Chartist leaders frequently disagreed with one
another (see Picture Gallery on page 18 for a summary). These disagreements were frequently tinged with genuine personal dislike. Two of
the most impressive of the leaders, Feargus O'Connor and William
Lovett, loathed what the other stood for. The following is a very thinly
veiled attack made by Lovett on O'Connor in a speech in 1845:

◢ Source 6

We are persuaded that numbers of you have been deceived by sophistry [cunning and deceptive arguments], and led by falsehood to injure the cause you have so warmly espoused. We seek to call you back to reason ... Judging from their conduct towards the middle, the trading and commercial classes, persons might be led to suppose that the Charter was some exclusive working class measure, giving licence for abuse, threats and violence, instead of a measure of justice for uniting all classes in holy brotherhood and for promoting the common good of all ... Be assured that those who flatter your prejudices, commend your ignorance, and administer to your vices, are not your friends. 'Unwashed faces, unshorn chins' and dirty habits, will in no wise prepare you for political and social equality with the decent portion of your brethren ... Empty boastings, abusive language, and contempt for all mental and moral qualifications, will rather retard than promote your freedom; nay, even if you possessed political power, would still keep you the slaves and puppets of those who flourish by popular ignorance.

W. Lovett, **Life and Struggles of William Lovett** (1876; Garland, 1984)

O'Connor never forgave Lovett for establishing his National Association for the Moral, Social and Political Improvement of the People. The rules of this association made it quite clear that Lovett was sticking closely to the objectives of the London Working Men's Association. Education for citizenship remained central to Lovett's vision:

◢ Source 7

First,   To unite, in one general body, persons of all CREEDS, CLASSES and OPINIONS, who are desirous to promote the political and social improvement of the people.

Second,   To create and extend the principles of the PEOPLE'S CHARTER, and by every just means secure its enactment; so that the industrious classes may be placed in possession of the franchise, the most important step to all political and social reformation.

Third,   To create PUBLIC HALLS of SCHOOLS FOR THE PEOPLE, throughout the kingdom ... Such halls to be used during the day as INFANT, PREPARATORY, and HIGH SCHOOLS, in which the children shall be educated on the most approved plans the association can devise ... and used of an evening for PUBLIC LECTURES on physical, moral and political science; for READINGS, DISCUSSIONS, MUSICAL ENTERTAINMENTS, DANCING and such other healthful and rational recreations as may serve to instruct and cheer the industrious classes after their hours of toil, and prevent the formation of vicious and intoxicating habits.

Fourth, To establish ... NORMAL or TEACHERS' SCHOOLS, for the purpose of instructing schoolmasters and mistresses in the most approved systems of physical, mental, moral and political training.

Fifth, To establish, on the most approved system, such AGRICULTURAL and INDUSTRIAL SCHOOLS as may be required for the education and support of the orphan children of the association.

Sixth, To establish CIRCULATING LIBRARIES, from a hundred to two hundred volumes each, containing the most useful works on politics, morals, the sciences, history, and such instructive and entertaining works as may be generally approved of ... Such libraries to vary as much as possible from each other, and to be sent in rotation from one town or village in the district to another ...

Extracts from the **Plan, Rules and Regulations of the National Association of the United Kingdom**, 1841

This plan was vigorously attacked in *Northern Star* as an unwelcome 'New Move'. O'Connor wrote a number of articles criticising it as destroying Charter unity and he used his great authority within the National Charter Association to solicit responses from local societies which also condemned it. They were not slow in coming and they, too, were eagerly reprinted in *Northern Star*. In the northern industrial areas, particularly, Lovett and Collins's initiative was overwhelmingly condemned as deflecting the movement from its main task. Moreover, as Reverend George Harrison, the delegate for Nottingham, told the 1842 Chartist National Convention, all of the educational and cultural benefits which the 'New Move' advocated had already been put in place. Lovett's initiative was, therefore, literally useless.

Dr Peter McDouall also issued a pamphlet in which he attacked William Hill, editor of *Northern Star*, over his views about the strikes of 1842. McDouall, on behalf of the executive of the National Charter Association, had proposed, and carried, a resolution making the achievement of the People's Charter a central aim of the strike. Hill had argued that this decision – the responsibility of 'a few hot-headed and short-sighted men' – was folly. It invited massive retaliation from the authorities and a struggle which 'the people' would be bound to lose. McDouall's attack on Hill is significant. It shows the depth of division among Chartist leaders over tactics at the time and it also provides a clear statement of the class antagonism which motivated many of them. McDouall made clear that his targets included not only the aristocracy, the traditional focus of artisan radical attack, but also the middle-class employers engaged in their own struggle to repeal the Corn Laws:

◢ Source 8

He is a fool who knows nothing of men and men's ways; and who thinks that the charter alone would have defeated the masters. The capitalists, with the corn law agitation, will beat the chartist party asleep; but the chartists awake, with the charter, will beat all the schemes which self-interest ever set afloat to delude and humbug society ... Had we merely gone to a public meeting, and delivered ourselves of ... cautions and warnings, we would have succeeded as well as if we had scolded the ocean or tried to reason the waves into obedience. Nothing but the cold steel will at times decide a victory; and nothing saved us from utter defeat save the cry for the higher, the more glorious prize, of the people's charter. The allegiance of a chartist population [in Manchester] was almost destroyed, until, high above all other cries, arose the overwhelming one for the good old cause ...

[Then] the bread and cheese sympathy [of the Anti-Corn Law League] existed no longer – the cheap loaf and the beggar's dish went off in each other's company – the apostles vanished behind the scenes to prepare their new characters, whose costume was to be characterised by the soldier's jacket, the constable's baton, and the magistrate's warrant ...

To sum up the case ... We had two parties in opposition to us – the capitalists and the aristocracy. The jealousy subsisting between those parties constituted our strength and forbade their union. We had two evils to guard against; the first was, not to strengthen the capitalists; the second was, not to protect the landlords ...

[Our] only true policy was to assume a perfectly peaceful, but thoroughly united, and steady front, so that we should not alarm the middle classes or frighten the capitalists and aristocracy into a coalition for mutual defence ... Had we adopted the only just and consistent medium I have pointed out ... we might have succeeded without much danger; and had we failed, we would have failed without loss, and certainly without any disgrace. We wanted [lacked] knowledge, honesty, union and peace ... The usual *fatality was in attendance on the strike. Division was carefully stirred up, jealousies were fomented, and dark suspicions launched against those who were advocates of the political movement; all the artillery of low intrigue and secret cabal were used unsparingly to damn the movement by suspicion, wrangling, uncertainty and fear.*

Peter McDouall, **Letter No. 1 to the Manchester Chartists** *(1842)*

Case study: The leadership of Feargus O'Connor

During his career, Feargus O'Connor fell out with virtually every other national Chartist leader. Most hated what they called his 'dema- goguery' – his direct, frequently emotional, appeals to the masses. Some noted that he never had an original thought. Others thought that he badly misled his followers by suggesting that a physical-force strategy could work. George Julian Harney had called for 'physical force' in 1838 and 1839; after 1842 he had second thoughts:

◢ Source 9

As to what O'C[onnor] has been saying lately about 'physical force', I think nothing of it. The English people ... applaud it at public meetings, but that is all. Notwithstanding all the talk in 1839 about 'arming', the people did not arm, and they will not arm ... The body of the English people, without becoming a slavish people, are becoming an eminently pacific [peaceful] people ... To attempt a 'physical-force' agitation at the present time would be productive of no good but on the contrary of some evil.

Letter from George Julian Harney to Friedrich Engels, 30 March 1846, quoted in E. Royle, **Chartism** *(Addison Wesley Longman, 1996)*

Unlike other leaders, however, Harney did retain respect for Feargus, praising his tolerance of others' views and his willingness to have those views expressed in his own newspaper. He also noted that a 'popular chief' should have 'a magnificent bodily appearance, an iron frame, eloquence' and 'possess great animal courage, contempt of pain and death'. O'Connor had all these attributes and, Harney concluded, if he were metaphorically 'thrown overboard, we might go further and fare worse'.

Others were far less charitable. Those who considered themselves from the 'thinking', artisan end of Chartism were especially critical of the way in which O'Connor manipulated crowds to satisfy his own leadership ambitions. When in Newcastle early in 1839, Robert Lowery was impressed by the local leadership shown by Augustus Beaumont and was clearly influenced by his opinion of O'Connor:

◢ Source 10

I … found his [Beaumont's] keen perception of men had at once read the character of O'Connor. 'O'Connor is not to be trusted,' said he; 'He's a coward, and if ever we should have to fight he is not to be depended on …' I knew little of O'Connor then, but often thought of these words when after events showed their truth …

Politically, Feargus O'Connor was the popular man in Yorkshire and Lancashire, and in every district he was beginning to attract the admiration of the unthinking crowd, while the few far-seeing already perceived the deficiencies of his character, and the evil results that his language would eventually lead to … He went down into the factory districts, and speaking to please he soon became popular … He was no reasoner, saw no deeper than the surface of things, and looked no farther than the next moment for the effects of a present action … His vanity and self-esteem were diseased, and upset all the rest of his powers.

R. Lowery, Passages in the Life of a Temperance Lecturer (1856–67) in B. Harrison and P. Hollis (eds), **Robert Lowery: Radical and Chartist** (Europa Publications, 1979)

William Lovett complained about O'Connor's 'Irish braggadoccio about arming and fighting'. His bitterness was also evident in his comments on O'Connor's response to his launching of the National Association for the Moral, Social and Political Improvement of the People in 1841:

◢ Source 11

His speech [at Birmingham in 1839] … about 'fleshing swords to the hilt' … furnished our opponents with a daily text, and a keen weapon with which to assail us …

This Proposal [for the National Association], while it was warmly greeted by the Press, and received the commendations of a great number of intelligent minds among all parties, was met with falsehood, intolerance and bitterest rancour, by the most prominent organ of Chartism, Northern Star. Its proprietor and editor jointly denounced it … as a plan intended to destroy Feargus O'Connor's political supremacy and subvert *one which he had previously concocted. Education was ridiculed, Knowledge was sneered at, Facts were perverted, Truth suppressed and the lowest passions and prejudices of the multitude were appealed to ... We were denounced ... as 'thieves, liars and traitors to the cause of Chartism', as persons who 'if a guillotine existed in England would be its just victims'.*

W. Lovett, **Life and Struggles of William Lovett** (1876; Garland, 1984)

Chartism's first historian took a similar line:

◢ Source 12

O'Connor ... did not depend alone upon physical strength for the involuntary respect in which he was held by the multitude. His broad massive forehead ... bore evidence ... of great intellectual force. To assert that he possessed a mind solid and steady were to say too much, no man with an equal amount of intellect were ever more erratic. Had the solidity of judgement been equal to his quickness of perception he would intellectually have been a great man, but this essential quality of greatness he lacked, hence his life presents a series of mistakes and contradictions, which, as men reflected more, lowered him in their estimation.

R. G. Gammage, **History of the Chartist Movement, 1837–54** (1894; Merlin Press, 1969)

Until the 1980s, these early judgements about O'Connor were mostly confirmed by historians (see Chapter 5). Recently, however, he has been rehabilitated as the central force which drove Chartism on in the difficult days of the 1840s. David Jones, the most balanced and perceptive of the historians of Chartism, attempted to explain why O'Connor had so long been undervalued:

◢ Source 13

Resentment is at the heart of early Chartist history. Broken hopes and injured pride turned memoirs into thinly disguised denunciations of Chartist leadership. Men who had always been wary of excessive hero-worship attacked O'Connorites for their exaggerated claims of popular support, their obstructionism and inconsistencies, and their willingness to divide the Chartist body and plunge the country into revolution.

D. Jones, **Chartism and the Chartists** (Allen Lane, 1975)

Jones praised O'Connor's perception and the way he used Chartist National Conventions to keep the big issues at the forefront of debate.

J. Epstein's study of O'Connor plainly sought to right a number of historiographical wrongs and the political sympathies of its author are clear:

◢ Source 14

Chartism was a class movement. It was O'Connor's insistence upon the need to construct and maintain an independent working-class movement which won him the respect of working-class radicals ... As an organiser and agitator ... he made his greatest contribution to the Chartist movement. O'Connor's significance derived not from the originality of his political ideas, but rather from the extent to which he came to embody the ideas of an established radical tradition and from his ceaseless efforts to give these ideas organisational and agitational form within real situations of political struggle ...

With remarkable forbearance, energy and enthusiasm, O'Connor battled to overcome the divisions and sources of fragmentation within the working-class movement ... Following the defeats of 1839 and early 1840, Chartism lost much of its earlier sense of urgency ... The vulnerability of Chartism's national unity was tested. Both from outside and within the Chartist ranks the movement was faced with a series of 'rival' or alternative agitations. O'Connor's leadership was crucial in determining the Chartist reaction, at both the local and national level.

*J. Epstein, **The Lion of Freedom** (Croom Helm, 1982)*

Dorothy Thompson's incisive series of essays, collected together in the form of a book, went even further:

◢ Source 15

Of the importance of Feargus O'Connor as a national leader, there can ... be no question ...

In fact, so far from being the exploiter and distorter of the Chartist movement, O'Connor was so much at the centre of it that, had the name Chartist not been coined, the radical movement between 1838 and 1848 must surely have been called O'Connorite Radicalism. Remove him and his newspaper from the picture, and the movement fragments, localises and loses its continuity ...

He was a shrewd and capable politician and a not inconsiderable organiser and administrator in addition ... O'Connor was the national figure whose visits were the occasion to organise massive demonstrations, to exploit every theatrical device, from the unhitching of his carriage outside the town to the massive display of numbers, banners, tableaux, and music at the gathering point of the rally. Napier spoke of mass meetings at which the crowds melted away once O'Connor had finished speaking, and there is no doubt that no other figure ever produced the same turn out ... He was always the gentleman demagogue making no attempt to present himself as 'ordinary'.

D. Thompson, **The Chartists: Popular Politics in the Industrial Revolution** *(Temple Smith, 1984)*

In a modern phrase, O'Connor was an image-conscious, style politician.

One of the most recent studies of nineteenth-century radicalism stressed O'Connor's massive contribution to what might be called Chartist culture:

◢ Source 16

The National Charter Association was the cornerstone of a democratic counter-culture of Chartist schools, stores, chapels, burial clubs, temperance societies and other facilities for education, recreation and the celebration of radical anniversaries ...

A grassroots complement to political struggle, branch culture held the movement together during the lean periods, preserving the structure intact and in readiness for the return of excitement and the next great national agitation ... A tireless promoter of the new organisation, O'Connor strongly approved of collective self-help within the democratic and inclusive framework of the National Charter Association. What he opposed was divisive elitism, the establishment of exclusive standards of Chartist membership, the withdrawal from mass action, developments which led back to the middle-class embrace.

J. Belchem, **Popular Radicalism in Nineteenth-century Britain** *(Macmillan, 1996)*

Such forceful and cogently argued tributes from distinguished scholars of radical politics at the very least deserve respect. O'Connor's reputation now stands higher than ever before. But has he recently been overpraised? It is a normal pattern in the creation of historical interpretations that, when one is overturned, the reinterpretation goes too far in the opposite direction. Is this the case with O'Connor? You must study the evidence above for yourself, link it to your wider knowledge of Chartism and come to a judgement. How you judge will probably reflect your overall view about the importance of Chartism because – like him or loathe him – O'Connor was the most powerful, if not the most able, leader the movement had.

Remember two things as you go about the task:

◢ the latest interpretation is not necessarily the most convincing
◢ a historical judgement is not the same as the summing up by a judge in a criminal trial: a dispassionate consideration of all relevant evidence, leaving all the key questions open to the jury (not that judges actually match up to this ideal very often!) Like the historians quoted above, you should aim for some well-reasoned and well-supported partiality!

This book itself presents an interpretation about Chartism, of course. The author has done a fair bit of rummaging around Chartist sources himself over the years. His own judgement on O'Connor, for what it is worth, is less favourable than that of the historians quoted above. He takes more note of the collective weight of contemporary opinion and of the fact that virtually every other Chartist leader found plenty to complain about in O'Connor. They were not all motivated by spite and frustrated ambition! Also, so much of this attempted rehabilitation, it seems to this author, comes from a position of sympathy (perhaps extreme sympathy in some cases) with the idea that there existed during the 1840s a collective working class, whose interests were clearly distinct from those of other social groups, which O'Connor was trying to keep together to force the People's Charter from the reluctant grip of the authorities. But if there was no such collective working class, was his strategy sensible? Many in the skilled working classes who had fallen out with O'Connor and many in the radically-inclined middle classes sought to bring combined pressure on the authorities and to win victories in stages. A frontal assault, as Lovett, Collins and Harney all knew before 1848, was bound to fail. Ultimately, it was the Lovett strategy which brought about the political changes O'Connor wanted, though certainly not in the way O'Connor wanted them to be brought about.

Effective leadership?

Every political organisation strives for unity and is weakened by splits. The splits within the Chartist leadership over ideology and tactics were deep and they had important consequences. Should we, however, conclude that they were vital in explaining why the People's Charter was not achieved? Another way of looking at Chartist leadership starts with a recognition of the scale of the challenge faced. As David Jones put it: 'The task of bringing together men with varying levels of political and social consciousness was an enormous one.'

If we start from the presumption that the People's Charter could not have been won except by successful revolution and that the conditions for successful revolution did not exist, then our evaluation of Chartist leadership becomes very different. We concentrate less on why Chartist leaders let their followers down by failing to get the People's Charter passed, and much more on what those leaders, both central and local, actually achieved. The following points, not a complete list, support the view that Chartist leadership – diverse, squabbling, vain and over-ambitious as it certainly was – did not fail. It was much more effective than is generally allowed.

1 Chartist organisation, in terms of arranging meetings, lectures and a range of public events, was extremely efficient. Though few admit it, it rivalled that of the Anti-Corn Law League.

2 It produced popular journalism of the highest order, which both informed and educated. It transformed the confidence and expectations of working people. Any comparison between the Chartist press of the 1840s and the popular press of the 1990s is embarrassingly, pathetically, to the disadvantage of the latter. Rarely has there been a starker demonstration of the historical truism that 'change does not necessarily equal progress'.

3 It responded to a number of reverses (notably in 1839 and 1842) with courage, ingenuity and resilience, refusing to accept defeats as final. The flame of radical resource burned bright throughout the Chartist period.

4 The different routes to self-knowledge and 'improvement' which widely-read Chartist leaders put forward were at least as much a strength as a weakness. Political messages continued to be put powerfully across.

5 The work of the leaders transformed the culture of huge numbers of working people, whether through 'Christian Chartism', 'Education Chartism', 'Temperance Chartism' or just in the meetings and social gatherings arranged at local level. These cultural forms helped to develop not only confidence but a sense of collective identity. The process was far from completed by the end of the 1840s but without the vision and initiative of Chartist leaders it would have taken much longer, if it had occurred at all.

6 Perhaps most important of all, Chartist leadership (albeit in different ways and with very different emphases) rose to the challenge of transforming artisan radicalism into something both broader and deeper. Artisan radicalism's essentially political message was yoked more effectively than ever before to the rapidly changed social and economic needs of working people in an urban, industrial culture. As we shall see in Chapter Four and Chapter Six, the evolution of Chartism had consequences which were to transform the organisations and culture of working people in the second half of the century.

TASKS

Working with sources

The sources in this chapter provide evidence about Chartist leadership. It may be appropriate to work in three separate groups, as indicated below. Each group should read through the relevant sources:

⬛ first, make sure that you understand what is being said

⬛ second, try to relate what is said to your wider knowledge about Chartism.

Different groups should report back their findings to the class as a whole.

Group 1

Group 1 should work with Mark Hovell's assessment of Chartist leadership (Source 1, pages 60–61) and link this to William Lovett's speech of 1845 (Source 6, page 65).

Questions

a On what grounds did Chartists at the Chartist National Convention of 1839 justify their use of the title 'M.C.' [Member of the Convention]?

b With which group, 'the preachers of violence' or 'the preachers of peaceful agitation', does Hovell seem to be in sympathy? How, from the evidence of this source, can you tell?

c Would Hovell have agreed with the points made in Lovett's speech of 1845? Explain your answer by reference to both sources.

Group 2

Group 2 should work with Peter McDouall's letter to the Manchester Chartists (Source 8, pages 67–68).

Questions

a Why does McDouall say that 'the charter alone' would not have been enough to defeat the masters?

b What was the meaning of McDouall's reference to 'cold steel'?

c Explain what McDouall meant by his reference to the enemies of the Chartists preparing 'new characters'.

d Using this document, what were McDouall's criticisms of Chartist tactics during the 1842 strike?

Group 3

Group 3, which might be the largest group, should work with the sources which evaluate O'Connor's leadership (Sources 9–16). One sub-group should concentrate on contemporary opinions of O'Connor (Sources 9–12, pages 68–70), answering questions (a) and (b). The other should concentrate on more modern assessments (Sources 13–16, pages 70–72), answering questions (c) and (d). Question (e) should be tackled by the group as a whole.

a List the criticisms which are made of O'Connor in Sources 9–12.

b Which of the authors of Sources 9–12 appears to be most bitter and most personally motivated? Justify your choice by reference to all four sources.

c List the strengths of O'Connor's leadership, as identified by the modern historians (Sources 13–16).

d Which of the authors of Sources 13–16 appears to be most enthusiastic about O'Connor's leadership? Justify your choice by reference to all four sources.

e Why do you think the contemporary assessments differ so much from the modern ones? Can you infer anything about the likely reliability of these assessments from the nature of their conclusions?

CHAPTER FOUR

HOW MUCH CHANGE DID CHARTISM UNDERGO IN THE YEARS 1838 TO 1851?

Objectives

◢ To examine why, and to what extent, the strength and the aims of the Chartist movement changed from the origins of the movement to the aftermath of the last mass outbreak in 1848

◢ To understand the reasons for these changes

◢ To examine relations between working people and the middle classes during the Chartist era

◢ To evaluate and interpret contemporary source material by understanding it, extracting information from it and reaching conclusions.

There are no statistics by which we can reliably measure changes in support for Chartism. However, it is clear that support fluctuated substantially, with three peaks in 1838–39, 1842 and 1848. In between, mass support dropped off and the movement's effectiveness was further reduced by splits within the movement (see Part 1 and Chapter 3). One rough and ready way to indicate the scale of the peaks and troughs, however, is by using estimates of sales for *Northern Star*, by far the movement's most influential publication. The sales estimates cannot be used as a measure of membership or support, since far more people supported Chartism than could buy, or in some cases even read, *Northern Star*. They measure relative strength and weakness only.

Fluctuating though they are, these are impressive figures. In most years, *Northern Star* outsold virtually all provincial newspapers written for the middle and upper classes. It made a major cultural contribution to working-class life, especially in Lancashire and Yorkshire, for more than a decade.

Relations with the middle classes

In the long history of radical agitation against the system of aristocratic government, informal, and sometimes formal, co-operation between the middle classes and artisan groups had been vitally important. As

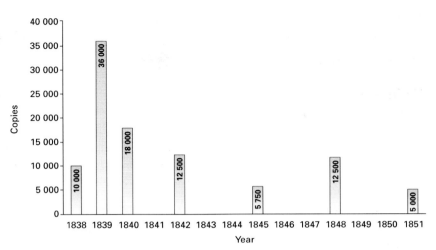

Table 1 Sales figures for *Northern Star*

we have seen (Chapter 1), that co-operation took a savage knock with the passage of the 1832 Reform Act, but it was not destroyed. The origins of Chartism cannot be understood except as the culmination of a long movement by those who called themselves the 'useful' or 'productive' classes against the 'useless'.

We should also remember that, both before the industrial revolution and long after it in trades which were not heavily mechanised, there was no large social gulf between skilled workers and small master manufacturers. Indeed, many readily made the transition from one group to the other. The example of Francis Place is instructive. The 'radical tailor of Charing Cross' who, as a journeyman breeches-maker, had been associated with the radical London Corresponding Society of the 1790s, had by the 1820s become a respectable shopkeeper and master tailor who helped to secure the repeal of the Combination Acts in 1824. By this, trade unions regained their legal status. In the mid-1830s, working with the London Working Men's Association, he helped draft the People's Charter. Few artisans became as nationally prominent as Place, of course, but he represented a very important type. Many artisans had realistic aspirations for social improvement which would see them raised into the middle classes. The frustration of these ambitions by changes in the organisation of industry and by economic depression was the midwife of Chartism. Whatever Chartism *became*, its origins were far from class-conscious. The impetus for improvement never left the skilled workers either:

◢ Source 1

Denounce the middle classes as you may, there is not a man among you worth halfpenny a week that is not anxious to elevate himself among them.

> James Ackland, a lecturer for the Anti-Corn Law League, 1840, quoted in D. Jones, **Chartism and the Chartists** (Allen Lane, 1975)

Ackland, a skilful orator, knew well how to play on weaknesses and this brief extract from a speech to Sheffield Chartists implies that hostility between the artisan and middle classes was recent. The reduction in opportunity for skilled workers to become manufacturers was at least as important as alleged 'class-consciousness' in explaining why relations between the Chartists and the Anti-Corn Law League were generally so cool. By the 1840s, the radical bookseller James Leach confirmed this; he also alluded to a deeper truth. Those who had been able to improve their status, but who still felt vulnerable to pressure from below, were likely to be the keenest defenders of their position, if necessary by oppressing workers.

◢ Source 2

[He] denied the assertion that the interests of the middle and the working classes were identical ... Those who but a short time had been lifted out of the puddle hole were the greatest tyrants.

> James Leach, quoted in D. Jones, **Chartism and the Chartists** (Allen Lane, 1975)

It is often assumed that relations between skilled workers and small master manufacturers were closer in towns which did not in the 1830s and 1840s have large factories. The pre-eminent 'workshop' city was, of course, London with its huge range of trades. More typical large towns were Birmingham and Sheffield – metal communities with a strong artisan tradition and dominated by workshops. Birmingham produced the best-known 'political union' of the middle and working classes to generate pressure for the Reform Act in the early 1830s. The Birmingham Political Union remained active after 1832, still led by the successful banker Thomas Attwood. Like Henry Hetherington (see page 20), Attwood complained that the Reform Act had gone nowhere near far enough. The Birmingham Political Union still maintained the crucial distinction between the 'productive' and 'unproductive' classes. For Attwood, even after the Reform Act, 'the concept of the "productive" or "industrious" classes united labour and capital, and defined their common interests against a landed and moneyed aristocracy invested with political power through an unrepresentative Parliament' (C. Behagg, 'An alliance with the middle class' in J. Epstein & D. Thompson (eds), *The Chartist Experience* (Macmillan, 1982)).

Behagg believes, however, that this formula had begun to wear thin in Birmingham even before the Chartist National Convention of 1839. The reform of local government, begun by the Municipal Corporations Act in 1835, gave the middle classes power and influence in local politics which they had previously been denied. Some Chartists resented what they saw as increasing middle-class 'withdrawal' from democratic politics after the first municipal elections in Birmingham in 1838. A separate working-class committee in Birmingham published the following poem in early 1839 which, while drawing on older radical tradition of 'liberty' and patriotism against a corrupt government, also spoke the language of class-consciousness:

◢ Source 3

Britons arise and yet be free
Demand your rights and liberty
Tyrants long have shared the spoil,
The Working Class share all the toil
Now! Or never! Strike the blow!
Exert yourselves and crush the foe!

Quoted in C. Behagg, 'An alliance with the middle class' in
J. Epstein and D. Thompson (eds), **The Chartist Experience:**
Studies in Working-class Radicalism and Culture (Macmillan, 1982)

The Birmingham Political Union, perhaps the strongest radical force for moderation and 'moral-force' during the 1830s, collapsed under the strains placed on it during the Chartist National Convention of 1839. In the Chartist National Convention, the power balance, at least in terms of language and rhetoric, shifted from 'moral-force' to 'physical-force'. In the process, it either alarmed or demoralised 'moral-force' men. Nominations to the Chartist National Convention revealed that the middle classes were quite strongly represented. According to William Lovett's analysis:

◢ **Source 4**

The number of delegates composing the Convention was fifty-three ... Of this number three were magistrates, six newspaper editors, one clergyman of the Church of England, one Dissenting minister, and two doctors of medicine, the remainder being shopkeepers, tradesmen and journeymen.

W. Lovett, **Life and Struggles of William Lovett** (1876; Garland, 1984)

One or two of Lovett's 'tradesmen' were, in reality, even more established than his description would suggest. Patrick Matthew, for example, was both a prosperous grain-dealer and a landowner in Perthshire. More typical, perhaps, was George Rogers, a tobacconist from Bloomsbury (central London).

Discussions about what to do if parliament rejected the People's Charter however, revealed splits in, and defections from, the Chartist National Convention (see Chapter 3). The vicar of Warwick, Dr Wade, resigned at the end of March and most of the Birmingham delegates followed. The convention dissolved itself in September 1839 after further internal disputes and an attempt to force the authorities to grant the People's Charter by holding a 'sacred month' of strikes which it was forced to abandon when it became clear that there was insufficient support in the industrial areas. The response of John Richards, the shoemaker delegate from the Potteries, was typical of many:

◢ **Source 5**

My opinion ... is that the Sacred Month cannot in common providence be attempted here, there are rash spirits who would plunge head first into it, but the Majority will not move, so that I cannot think it is prudent for it to be Ordered at least for the present.

Letter from John Richards to T. R. Smart, 8 August 1839, quoted in R. Fyson, 'Homage to John Richards', in O. Ashton, R. Fyson and S. Roberts (eds), **The Duty of Discontent: Essays for Dorothy Thompson** (Mansell, 1995)

The most significant Chartist challenge in 1839, of course, was the Newport rising of 4 November. It was easily put down (see Part 1) but the event shows how the rejection of the People's Charter helped to push Chartists more towards physical force. Its leader, John Frost, was a tailor and draper who became a moderately prosperous tradesman. He had also been both Mayor of Newport and a magistrate. In the 1820s and early 1830s he had been a prominent supporter of universal suffrage and opponent of the corruption of the leading landed families of south Wales. After the rising collapsed, he and his two principal collaborators, Zephaniah Williams and William Jones, were at first sentenced to death. In February 1840, after some further violence (see Chronology of important events, page 6) and amid rumours of much more, the government was able to use convenient legal technicalities to cast doubt on some aspects of their trial. The three were instead reprieved and their sentences commuted to transportation. They were shipped, almost in panicky haste, to Australia. Frost returned to Britain, still bitterly hostile to the authorities, in 1856; the other two settled in Australia resentfully.

The first wave of Chartism, therefore, brought three important changes:

- the alienation of many middle-class supporters from the violence, and the threats of violence, which had accompanied Chartist activity. After 1839, Chartism became more purely a movement of discontented working classes than before
- the destruction of whatever fragile unity the movement possessed. The split between O'Connor and Lovett over the 'new move' (see pages 64–66) was obvious and deeply damaging, but there were divisions within the National Charter Association after 1841 also, despite O'Connor's attempt to use the NCA as a means of preserving unity
- the more extensive use of physical-force language. Once it became clear that the power of rational argument would not come near persuading the House of Commons to make major steps in the direction of democracy, then the language of coercion – strikes, 'exclusive dealing', calls for arming and drilling, and even revolution – became dominant.

The Anti-Corn Law League and the Complete Suffrage Movement

We have been looking at change within the Chartist movement. It is important to note elements of continuity as well. Perhaps the most important of these is the abiding distrust which most Chartists held for the middle classes throughout the late 1830s and the 1840s.

The Anti-Corn Law League, founded in Manchester by wealthy industrialists in 1839, had as its objective the repeal of the Corn Laws. Since the Corn Laws placed heavy duties on the import of corn, thus increasing the price of bread, it might be thought that the middle and working classes had a common interest in calling for their removal. Most manufacturers wanted free trade and the Corn Laws represented the biggest obstacle to its achievement. Working people wanted cheap bread to which the Corn Laws were also a major obstacle. Not surprisingly, the Anti-Corn Law League made many attempts to win working-class leaders' support for their campaign. These were nearly all rebuffed. The reason is not far to seek. After their experience in 1832, and also after the legislation of the 1830s which (so many working people thought) favoured the middle classes at the expense of working people, trust had broken down. The dominant mood is perhaps best captured by the Tyneside shoemaker John Mason addressing Chartists in Leicester in 1840:

◢ Source 6

Not that Corn Law Repeal is wrong; when we get the Charter we will repeal the Corn Laws and all the other bad laws. But if you give up your agitation for the Charter to help the Free Traders, they will not help you to get the Charter. Don't be deceived by the middle classes again. You helped them to get their votes ... But where are the fine promises they made you? Gone to the winds! They said when they had gotten their votes, they would help you to get yours. But they and the rotten Whigs have never remembered you. Municipal Reform has been for their benefit – not for yours. All other reforms the Whigs boast to have effected have been for the benefit of the middle classes – not for yours. And now they want to get the Corn Laws repealed – not for your benefit – but their own. 'Cheap Bread!' they cry. But they mean 'Low Wages'. Do not listen to their cant and humbug. Stick to your Charter. You are veritable slaves without your votes!

John Mason, quoted in A. Briggs (ed), **Chartist Studies** (Macmillan, 1959)

In 1841 and 1842, particularly, relations between the Anti-Corn Law League and Chartism were hostile. The Anti-Corn Law League tried to win working-class support which Chartist leaders resisted. So called 'Operative Anti-Corn Law Associations' were founded, aimed directly at working men. They had little success. Even in Sheffield, where relations between working people and the middle classes were relatively good, Chartist hostility to the League was clear. Richard Cobden recognised that the Anti-Corn Law League 'has eminently been a middle class agitation' and vulnerable to attack as such. Some Anti-Corn Law League meetings were broken up and Chartist newspapers poured out torrents of abuse on the malevolence and untrustworthiness of the League. Bronterre O'Brien was characteristically scathing:

◢ Source 7

Away, then, in God's name with all this talk about uniting with the middle classes ... That the middle class will not unite with us for the Charter is manifest. 'Tis equally clear that nothing short of Universal Suffrage will accomplish the changes we require; why waste breath, then, arguing whether we ought or ought not to unite with the middle classes?

Northern Star, *24 April 1841, quoted in P. Hollis (ed),* **Class and Conflict in Nineteenth-century England, 1815–50** *(Routledge, 1973)*

In 1842, many Chartists believed that the Anti-Corn Law League members who were manufacturing employers took the lead in goading workers to strike by reducing their wages. Strikes would lose the Chartists sympathy while, in the cotton districts at least, having mills lying idle during a slump in demand was far less damaging to manufacturers than strikes during boom conditions. Interestingly, in the years 1843 to 1846 when economic conditions improved and when the Anti-Corn Law League concentrated more of its efforts on winning support among tenant farmers in the agricultural areas, relations improved. In 1846, *Northern Star* carried an editorial which praised the prime minister, Sir Robert Peel, for introducing a bill to repeal the Corn Laws in the face of opposition from within his own party.

The Complete Suffrage Movement of 1842 was a deliberate attempt to bridge the widening gulf between middle and working classes around support for universal manhood suffrage. It was led by the Birmingham Quaker philanthropist Joseph Sturge. As a Quaker, he abhorred violence and sought reconciliation. He seems to have been liked by all the Chartist leaders with whom he came into contact. He even achieved the extraordinary feat of uniting Feargus O'Connor and William Lovett in their opinion of him. O'Connor called him 'a most excellent person'; Lovett praised his 'benevolent labours in the cause of humanity and freedom'. Lovett was, however, less enthusiastic about the reception the Complete Suffrage Movement received in the Chartist press:

◢ Source 8

This effort to effect a union between the two classes was to some extent successful; for a great many local Complete Suffrage Associations were formed in many towns. Great numbers of the working classes were, however, kept aloof from it, by the abuse and misrepresentations of the Northern Star.

W. Lovett, **Life and Struggles of William Lovett** (1876; Garland, 1984)

Lovett and O'Brien were among the Chartist leaders to attend a conference in Birmingham in April 1842 at which the Chartist 'Six Points' were formally adopted and significant disagreement turned only on whether the conference should formally commit itself to supporting 'the Charter' by name. Middle-class delegates would not go so far. When the conference reconvened at the end of December, O'Connor – in an exceedingly rare show of unity – actually seconded a motion proposed by Lovett which indicated that the People's Charter was central to all working-class agitation. It deserves to be more widely known:

◢ Source 9

That the Document entitled the People's Charter, embracing as it does all the essential details of a just and equal representation, couched in plain and definite language, capable of being understood by the great mass of the people ... and that the measure having been before the public for the last five years, forming the basis of the present agitation in favour of the suffrage, and for seeking to obtain the legal enactment of which vast numbers have suffered imprisonment, transportation, and death, it has, in the opinion of this meeting, a prior claim over all other documents proposing to embrace the principles of just representation.

W. Lovett, **Life and Struggles of William Lovett** (1876; Garland, 1984)

Sturge and his middle-class allies voted against the proposal which was carried only by Chartist votes. The Complete Suffrage Movement collapsed immediately. When one remembers that those middle-class figures prepared to have anything to do with the Complete Suffrage Movement represented the most conciliatory and accommodating elements, the validity of the Chartist perception that success could come only from within may readily be seen. Lovett could not resist a final dig which revealed the obstacles in the way of unity within the movement: 'I may state here my conviction that the split was not so much occasioned by the adverse vote, as from the strong resolve of the minority to have no fellowship with Fergus [sic] O'Connor.'

Another important strand of continuity in Chartism was the importance of the continued difficulties of skilled workers threatened by industrial change. In some places, this was so pronounced as to draw sympathy from unusual quarters. The editor of *Leicester Chronicle* (no friend to Chartism) commented on the widespread poverty of Leicester 'stockingers' (skilled stocking makers) in 1848:

◢ Source 10

We should not be surprised if, to a man, the framework knitters of this town and district were proved to be Chartists. In their ideas CHARTISM *... means a renovation of all things – a regeneration of the social state – a political millennium. It means better wages, limited hours of labour, comfort, independence, happiness – it means, in short, all that the fond heart of suffering man pictures to him of joy and prosperity in his happiest moments.*

Leicester Chronicle, *8 April 1848, quoted in J. F. C. Harrison,*
'Chartism in Leicester' in A. Briggs (ed), **Chartist Studies** *(Macmillan, 1959)*

Feargus O'Connor would have been hard-put to better this analysis of why Chartism was both a political and a social movement.

The Land Plan

O'Connor's Land Plan represents the most important Chartist initiative in the period between the collapse of the strikes in 1842 and the revival of Chartism at the end of 1847. It is often presented as a desperate throw of the dice by a man gambling with the lives of thousands of oppressed workers. It was an eye-catching idea aimed at maintaining Chartist unity at a time of trade revival and sharply diminished mass support. It offered, quite literally, a lottery winner's chance for the industrial worker to put behind him the horrors of industrial life and to embark on a new life as a farmer.

Three points need to be made to put matters in context:

1 Although his opponents in the movement criticised O'Connor's plan as a catchpenny trick to bolster the falling circulation of *Northern Star* (much as free offers and revelations of sexual scandals did for tabloid newspapers in the late twentieth century), he had been advocating 'back to the land' since the very beginning of the movement. Here he is addressing Chartists in Rochdale:

◢ Source 11

The people ought to have a portion of their native soil, and the poor squalid wretches who are put up in the close rooms and the noxious alleys of Manchester should have the power of turning out from them, and of enjoying the invaluable blessings of the sun and the air (Cheers) ... The land belonged to the people; those who by their labour and capital cultivated it have a right to its productions ... The labourers ought to possess the earth.

Northern Star, *13 July 1839, quoted in J. Epstein,*
The Lion of Freedom *(Croom Helm, 1982)*

2 Speeches such as the one quoted above were not new. They were commonplace among artisan radicals from the 1790s onwards. Indeed, they had been at the root of the objections of many of the religious radicals' vision of liberty for ordinary people during the English Civil War and Interregnum of the 1640s and 1650s. In the late eighteenth and early nineteenth century, Thomas Spence and his 'Spencean philanthropists' had revolutionary plans based on extensive land redistribution. O'Connor was tapping into a very old radical tradition, and trying to adapt it in practical ways for the new industrial age.

3 At the heart of O'Connor's plan was the structural imbalance between population and resources in an early industrial society. It is too easily forgotten that the population of Britain almost doubled

between 1801 and 1851 and that pressure on space became ever greater. O'Connor was trying to correct the balance between people living in town and in countryside. The government was meanwhile encouraging an increasing number of emigration schemes. These had considerable success. By the 1880s, of every 10 000 people, 58 in Scotland and 23 in England were emigrating (K.T. Hoppen, *The Mid-Victorian Generation, 1846–86*, Oxford University Press, 1998).

Perhaps, therefore, the land plan was not so far-fetched. The National Charter Association gave it enthusiastic backing in 1845 when the Chartist Land Co-Operative Society was founded. The name was changed to 'National Co-Operative Land Company' in 1847. A modern historian has explained how the land plan was to work:

◢ Source 12

A capital sum of £5 000 should be raised from 2 000 shares costing £2.10s (£2.50) each. Out of this, 120 acres of good arable land should be bought at the current price of £18.15s (£18.75) an acre. This would provide 60 cultivators with two acres each, and £2,250 would be left to build cottages and buy stock. These allotments would be let by the [land] company to members in perpetuity [for ever] for £5 per year, bringing in £300 per year as estate rent. This sum, sold at 20 years' purchase [the value calculated by multiplying the rent by the number of years], would raise £6,000, which would buy land for 72 cultivators. Their rent would bring in enough to buy land for 86, and so on. All the surplus industrial production could be removed from the slums and planted on the land by a process which only needed the energy and initiative of one man to start it, and he was there.

A. Hadfield, ***The Chartist Land Company*** *(David and Charles, 1970)*

The Chartist Land Co-Operative Society had a slow start but flourished briefly during the economic uncertainties of 1847, and changed its name to the National Co-Operative Land Company when the extraordinary sum of £77 000 was subscribed, mostly by skilled workers, dominated, as so often in Chartist ventures, by weavers and shoemakers. In all, about 70 000 people became members, especially strong support coming from Lancashire and Cheshire. Reality fell far short of expectation. Although a number of land settlements were established in 1847 and 1848 (see Chronology of important events, page 7), only about

250 people received settlements of two acres each. There was no shortage of critics among Chartist leaders. Bronterre O'Brien famously alleged that the scheme only 'extended the hellish principle of landlordism'. Others argued that it was a delusory form of escapism, deflecting Chartists from the main issue: improving life for the working classes in an increasingly urban society. Worse, the funds of investors were managed poorly and a succession of parliamentary enquiries eventually led to the National Co-Operative Land Company being dissolved by Act of Parliament in 1851.

Both contemporary critics and several later historians have used both the land plan and the collapse of the mass Chartist movement of April 1848 (see Chapter 6) as evidence that in its last phase the main change in Chartism was a loss of reality. Instead of concentrating on united protest, the movement chased shadows while its leaders bickered. Supporters of O'Connor, however, have pointed out that the land plan appeared for a time to be a viable initiative which gave Chartists, demoralised after the defeats of 1842, an alternative focus. Some have even suggested that, without the land plan, the Chartists would not have been able to mount their final challenge in 1848 at all.

Answering questions based on historical sources

Most source questions are designed to test your understanding of the material you are given. Although most sources are in prose, as extracts from books, letters, reports of speeches, etc., you may be asked to work with visual sources, with charts of statistics or even with verses and poems. The questions which follow relate to a variety of sources. In some of the questions, you will be asked to link your understanding of the sources to your own knowledge. You should become used to tackling questions with a particular focus or emphasis.

General hints in answering source or document questions

1 Always read your documents *slowly* and *carefully* at first to make sure that you understand them. When you start doing this, you may find the language unfamiliar. People in the past did not always speak or write as we do. You will get better at understanding as you gain experience and practice. Remember that part of your training as students of history involves 'getting inside' the period you are studying. This includes getting familiar with the material which has been left behind from that period for us all to study. Don't give up because some words, or phrases, are unfamiliar.

2 In answering document questions, you will almost certainly be asked not only to show understanding but also to draw conclusions. You may also be asked to comment on *how* the writer or speaker (or perhaps cartoonist or artist) is putting the message across.

3 You will be given information about the *origins* of a source – its *provenance,* to give it its technical name. This is designed to be used and can be as valuable to you as the material in the documents themselves. In the selection of sources within this chapter, you have speeches, a letter, a poem, newspaper articles and extracts from an autobiography. All of these sources will be

useful for something; they will also be more useful for some things than others! You can often use the provenance, linked to your knowledge of the context, to get vital clues to answering a document question.

4 Get used to doing *exactly* what you are asked – no more and no less. If you are told to use Document I, then do just that. You won't get marks for referring to Documents II or III, or for making extensive use of your own knowledge. On the other hand, if you are asked to use Documents III and IV 'and your own knowledge', you should understand that you need to select relevant material from the two documents named and relate this to your wider knowledge in order to answer the question you have been asked, which will usually be a 'judgement' question.

5 The questions below are for practice and no mark allocations have been given to them. In examinations, however, each subquestion will carry a maximum mark. The number of marks available almost always gives a strong clue as to how much you are expected to write. In most examinations, the number of marks builds up so that the last question is worth most. Make sure that you organise your time so that you leave plenty of time for the questions with most marks.

6 In examinations, most candidates get more marks on document, or source, questions. Examiners more readily give maximum marks for an exercise marked out of 3 or 4 than they do out of 20 or 25. You can do yourself a lot of good by remembering the basic rules relating to documents questions. Similarly, if you don't you will probably be throwing away marks on what most candidates consider the easier parts of the examination.

Source questions and hints on answering

Q1 *'Study Source 6. Why, according to this Source, does John Mason believe that Chartists should not join other organisations to get the Corn Laws repealed?'*

HINT: This question includes the phrase 'According to Source 6 ...' This indicates that all you need to answer the question will be found in that document. Don't use outside knowledge. The question is testing the skill of *comprehension*: can you understand why John Mason does not want Chartists to be heavily involved with the Corn Law question?

Q2 *'Study the sales figures for* Northern Star *(Table 1 page 79). What can you learn from it about changes in support for Chartism in the years 1838–51?'*

HINT: This question has a similar focus to Question 1. It requires you to understand what you see in one source. There are, however, two differences. One is obvious: this is a visual source and you need to get practice in making straightforward conclusions from charts, diagrams and the like. The second is not quite so obvious. The skill being tested is rather different. Here you are being asked to make a judgement based on presented material. The key skill is *inference*: can you work out a conclusion from material you are given in the examination? This builds on the skill of comprehension.

Q3 *'Study Source 3. How useful is this source as evidence about support for Chartism in 1839?'*

HINT: The focus of this question is *utility*. Like questions 1 and 2, you work with one source only, but you work on it in a different way. Here you are asked to make a judgement about the value of a source for a particular enquiry – in this case evidence about support for Chartism at a particular point. You will want to notice what kind of source this is (look at the text just above the source itself for further information), work out why it was likely to have been produced and what its likely audience was. In what ways does the content of the source help you towards understanding its usefulness? Try to avoid very general statements about utility; relate your answer to *this* source and the precise context required.

Q4 *'Do Sources 1 and 2 agree about relations between the middle classes and the working classes? Explain your answer.'*

HINT: This question asks you to match information from two sources and to provide a judgement based on evidence. You are being asked to make a *cross-reference* in order to reach a *judgement*. Both sources are short, so you won't have to do much reading. Nor are you asked to make use of any specific information from outside these two sources. You will notice, however, that the two sources don't answer one another directly, so you will need to do some working out for yourself.

Q5 *'What can you learn from Sources 7, 8 and 9 about the problems of making agreements about political reform between the middle and working classes?'*

HINT: The target here is similar to that for Question 5. You must *cross-refer* using the three sources. You are not required to use any further information but to answer the question you will need to make *inferences*. The precise phrasing of the question is crucial. Notice that here it says 'What can you learn?' It does *not* say 'How much can you learn?' or 'How well do these sources explain why those wanting to agree a programme of political reform between the middle and working classes had so much difficulty?' If you had been faced with either of these alternatives, you would need to make at least some reference to your wider knowledge of the subject.

Q6 *'Study Sources 9, 10 and 11 and use your own knowledge.*
"Chartism was a failure because its objectives were unrealistic and its leadership was weak."
On the evidence of these three sources, and using your own knowledge, how far do you agree with this assessment?'

HINT: Questions like this usually come last in a sequence of source questions and have the largest number of marks attached to them. They test your powers of *historical analysis*. They ask for a short essay in response, rather than the paragraph or so which will be enough for most other source questions. The question asks your views about a quotation. This quotation is very likely to have been made up by the examiner specifically to give you things both to agree and to disagree with before coming to an overall judgement. When answering questions like this remember:

◢ to use both the sources you are required to use *and* your own knowledge. If you miss out one or the other you could lose up to half the available marks

◢ to reach a clear judgement, but one which is sustainable from the evidence you have used

◢ since this is a big question, it might be a good strategy to *plan* your answer, just as you might a full essay. You should jot down the key points you want to make, remembering to produce some specific evidence to back each one up. In a task like this, three or four developed analytical points should be plenty. Then you should reach a reasoned judgement on whether or not you agree with the quotation. It's useful to remember that not everything about it is likely to be right. Fine-grained judgements get more marks than 'black or white' answers which simply seem to be agreeing (or disagreeing).

CHAPTER FIVE

INTERPRETING CHARTISM

Objectives

◢ To examine how, and why, interpretations of the nature and significance of Chartism have changed

◢ To evaluate a range of secondary source material, using it to show differences of emphasis and historical judgement about the Chartist movement.

Chartism has never lacked for historians. It was the most self-publicising popular movement in British history and the richness of source material in statements of belief, newspaper and other journal articles, reports of speeches and private correspondence offers inviting scope for the historian. It is not, therefore, so surprising that the first history of Chartism appeared within six years of the mass meeting on Kennington Common in 1848. It was written by R. G. Gammage, himself a Chartist with some very clear views about the deficiencies of Chartist leaders. Since 1854, the movement has been written about constantly and the spate of books and articles which appeared during the 1980s shows that its fascination as a subject for historical study has remained undimmed. This chapter gives you both a flavour of Chartist *historiography* and some evidence on which you can base your own enquiry.

KEY TERM

Historiography – the study of history writing, as opposed to history itself. It is concerned with interpretations about the past and how, and why, such interpretations came to be made. It frequently needs to explain why people come to very different views about the same event.

Gammage was a coachbuilder who also worked as a shoemaker before studying to become a physician. Anyone who reads his *History of the Chartist Movement, 1837–54* also becomes aware that he was a very capable writer. His narrative is lucid and he was able to use irony and sarcasm to considerable effect. He fits ideally that type of improving artisan, wedded to the acquisition of knowledge, most likely to find Feargus O'Connor's direct, and often emotional, appeals to working-class audiences distasteful. His book is by no means totally one-sided but it is clear that he believes Chartism to have been ill-served by its most prominent leader. His views on the controversy between the followers of O'Connor and those of Lovett in 1842 are clear enough:

◢ View 1

We must here observe that although no direct conspiracy might exist against the Executive [of the Complete Suffrage Movement – see Chapter 4], neither O'Connor nor any of his salaried servants exhibited a good feeling towards that body. It was not sufficiently O'Connor-ridden to suit the purposes of the [Northern] Star chamber; and although little was done openly against it, secret whisperings were at work to bring it into discredit … O'Connor never discountenanced any attacks made upon it, unless he saw that the wind of public support was blowing in its favour. This was almost always his public standard of right and wrong. He generally too, praised a man most enormously before he condemned him; thus leaving the more unreflecting to infer that his condemnation was a painful public duty … That O'Connor had a desire to make the people happier, we never in our lives disputed. He would have devoted any amount of work for that purpose; but there was only one condition on which he would consent to serve the people – that condition was, that he should be their master.

R. G. Gammage, **History of the Chartist Movement, 1837–54** *(1894 edition; Merlin Press, 1969)*

Much the most influential book on Chartism in the first half of the twentieth century was Mark Hovell's *The Chartist Movement*, published in 1918. It is, in many ways, an impressive book and is still worth reading for the clarity of its narrative (not a strong feature of some more recent writing) and for the care which it takes to link Chartism to the process of rapid industrial change. Hovell relied for his sources on Chartist autobiographies, on the extensive archive of the artisan-turned-master manufacturer, Francis Place, housed in the British Library, and on Chartist newspapers. Like so many history books written by progressive writers of the early twentieth century, he was concerned to explain progress. The achievement of democracy (much advanced in the year of publication by the extension of the franchise to all men and to women over 30 years of age) was a great advance in a civilised society. The Chartists aimed for democracy and so were agents of progress worthy of detailed study.

Hovell was realistic enough to recognise that 'not a single article of Chartist policy had the remotest chance of becoming law until the movement had expired', though his explanation for this gives a clue to his wider views. He continued: 'It was only when Chartism ceased to be a name of terror that the process of giving effect to its programme was taken up by the middle-class Parliaments of the later Victorian age.' The great British elite, therefore, would not give in to threats or to violence. Hovell's book is much more sympathetic to those leaders he considered to be the apostles of progress – such as Lovett, Vincent, Collins and Lowery – than he was to those he believed were misleading the masses. Pre-eminent among these, of course, was O'Connor. He is not unsympathetic to the ordinary working people who supported Chartism, but he pities their ignorance and shows contempt for physical-force leaders.

◢ View 2

[O'Connor] was well versed in all the arts of popularity, and could be all things to all men. With rough working men he was hail-fellow-well-met, but he could be dignified when it was necessary to make a more serious impression ... In Parliament he was a good House of Commons man and spoke more sensibly than many. To the London artisans he spoke as an experienced politician. In the North, among the fustian-jackets and unshorn chins [a phrase used by O'Connor himself to describe ordinary working men] he was the typical demagogue, unloading upon his unsophisticated hearers rigmaroles of absurdity and sedition, flavoured by irresistibly comic similes and anecdotes ... As a political thinker O'Connor was quite negligible. He was totally without originality in this respect and borrowed all his ideas ...

The great Chartist following had, we may safely say, no policy at all. It followed its leaders with touching devotion into whatsoever blind alleys they might go. The plain Chartists had nothing to contribute to Chartist doctrine. A moving sense of wrong, a fierce desire to remedy the conditions of their daily life, were the only spurs which drove them into agitation and rioting. Hence the incoherence and sincerity of the whole movement ...

To some Chartists the war of classes was the necessary condition of social progress, and their characteristic attitude was the refusal of all co-operation between working men and those who did not gain their bread by manual labour. To others of a more *practical temperament experience showed that it was wise to unite the proletariat with the enlightened middle classes in common bonds of interest and affection.*

M. Hovell, **The Chartist Movement** *(1918; Manchester University Press, 1970)*

O'Connor's *Northern Star* also attracted much more hostile criticism than has been given by any historian since. Readers acquainted with the *Sun* and *Star* at the end of the twentieth century will be astonished to learn that Hovell judged *Northern Star* thus:

It made no pretence at being an 'elevating' paper. Like many cheap papers today, it gave the public exactly what the public wanted ... [Francis] Place declared that Northern Star *had degraded the whole Radical Press. It was truly the worst and most successful of the Radical papers, a melancholy tribute to the low level of intelligence of its readers.*

M. Hovell, **The Chartist Movement** *(1918; Manchester University Press, 1970)*

The reference to Francis Place gives a strong clue as to why Hovell's interpretation met with such criticism from historians in the 1960s and 1970s. Later historians have argued that his interpretation has been damaged both by the London-based artisan sources he placed too much reliance upon and by his own 'improving' and 'progressive' prejudices. He understood, and sympathised with, those who clearly had similar values to his own. O'Connor did not – and suffered mightily in the pages of Hovell's book.

The most influential reaction to Hovell's account in the postwar era was the volume edited by Asa Briggs and published in 1959 as *Chartist Studies*. Taking the view that too much Chartist historiography had been dominated by overall national studies and, particularly, by an undue emphasis on the great national leaders, Briggs published a collection of essays by leading scholars of working-class history in the nineteenth century which focused mainly on Chartism in particular locations, including Manchester, Glasgow, Leeds, Leicester and (as a welcome rural case study) Suffolk. The collection amply demonstrated the wide regional diversity in Chartism and brought to light a number of local figures, mostly artisans, whose contribution had been almost totally ignored by earlier studies. The collection also confirmed how crucial to the emergence of Chartism were the important political and social struggles of the 1830s. Parliamentary reformers stood shoulder to shoulder with **Tory *humanitarians*** in the campaign for factory reform, and especially a 'ten-hours' Bill. There was also an unbroken transition from hostility to the New Poor Law into Chartism. The collection also helps us understand why there was so much more popular support for Chartism in the north of England than there was in London.

KEY TERM

Tory humanitarians were people, often from a privileged landed background, who believed that it was the duty of those with wealth to ensure that the interests of the poor were protected. Most opposed the values of free trade and *laissez-faire* held by many factory owners and supporters of industrial capitalism. Tory humanitarians were rarely political reformers – indeed, they looked backwards to idealised views about the situation before the industrial revolution upset things – but they often had interests in common with the reformers in the 1830s and 1840s.

Chartist Studies inspired a number of other local studies which greatly added to the stock of knowledge. During the 1960s and 1970s a number of research theses which took this localist approach were begun on both the implementation of the New Poor Law and on Chartism. Some resulted in useful publications. Local studies, nevertheless, emphasised an approach which many historians regretted. Some, and particularly those on the intellectual Marxist left, felt that the essential Chartist baby had been flushed down some localist plughole. It was all very well to study Chartism in Preston, Oldham or Halifax, but unless these local studies were integrated securely into the wider picture, they were of limited value. Chartism was, after all, a *national* movement. More, it was the biggest working-class movement in the nineteenth century and it richly deserved celebration as such.

Marxist historians, almost none of whom come from working-class backgrounds themselves, nevertheless rushed to 'rescue' their key working-class movement from the fragmentation (and, by implication, belittling) of localism. They produced a rich, and in many respects enormously impressive, vein of scholarship from a thoroughbred stable which includes Edward and, especially, Dorothy Thompson and

John Saville. Readers should nevertheless be on their guard against a romantic reconstruction of a Chartist past peopled by unsung working-class heroes struggling against massive odds. Those odds included both a powerful capitalist elite and a cunning and sophisticated British state clever enough to avoid creating political martyrs. This state was nevertheless armed to the teeth with frightening weapons of repression which they brandished menacingly in the direction of anyone (or at least anyone from the working classes) who breathed the dread word 'democracy'. The writing is immensely beguiling and it is underpinned by extraordinary knowledge grounded in a wide range of sources. In places, though, it teeters on the very edge of romantic stereotype. It offers working-class heroes of the left to set against those well-heeled champions of British military and naval triumph or of daring imperial expansion (Francis Drake, Nelson, Wellington, Cecil Rhodes and the rest) which 'orthodox' historiography used to set before an admiring nation before those angels of our contemporary popular culture – pop stars and self-indulgent princesses – took their place. For historians, it might be thought, both heroes and their modern contemporary counterparts, 'role-models', are best given a wide berth – or, rather, studied in depth rather than through an expensively-tailored, but essentially false and superficial 'image'.

Marxist and socialist historiography has attempted to rescue the reputation of O'Connor, seeing him not as a vain, crude demagogue who misled his supporters but as a true people's champion. Dorothy Thompson, who has argued that 'the history of Chartism has in the past been seen too much in terms of its leaders or its would-be leaders', nevertheless fails to see how Chartism could have functioned without O'Connor:

◢ View 3

In fact, so far from being the exploiter and distorter of the Chartist movement, O'Connor was so much the centre of it that, had the name Chartist not been coined, the radical movement between 1838 and 1848 must surely have been called O'Connorite Radicalism. Remove him and his newspaper from the picture, and the movement fragments, localises and loses its continuity ... No other leader or would-be leader in

*those years had the energy, ability, physique or charisma of Feargus O'Connor. For
good or ill, he was the main inspiration and guiding force of the movement.*

D. Thompson, **The Chartists: Popular Politics in the
Industrial Revolution** *(Temple Smith, 1984)*

James Epstein was in no doubt that it was 'for good'. He rejects the old
charge that O'Connor led Chartism astray and portrays him as a
far-sighted democrat who believed as fervently as Lovett and Collins
in the virtues of improvement, sobriety and respectability for
working men:

◢ View 4

*Working-class ignorance or insobriety was the result of social conditions, particularly
wage slavery, which only a total re-ordering of society could change. Universal
suffrage was the first necessary step on the road to working-class 'moral'
improvement. O'Connor's concern for Chartist intellectual and cultural goals has often
been ignored in assessments of his leadership, particularly, by the early historians of
Chartism who portrayed differences between O'Connor and Lovett as fundamental to
the development of national Chartist leadership. The central split in national leadership
in turn corresponded to a neat delineation in terms of working-class support: between
the 'physical-force' proletarians of the North – largely inarticulate, deferential and
motivated by economic distress – and the enlightened artisans of London – largely
articulate, independent and motivated by democratic idealism. That this picture of both
leadership and support is inaccurate and misconceived is one of the central
arguments of this study.*

J. Epstein, **The Lion of Freedom** *(Croom Helm, 1982)*

Such a reinterpretation needs to contend not only with a weight of
historiography before the 1980s, which was, as we have seen, overwhelmingly 'anti-Feargus' but also with the opinion of virtually all the
other Chartist leaders who saw, at the least, substantial flaws to accompany the massive presence. There also remain the charges that:

1 his indefatigable oratory raised unrealistic expectations throughout
   the country
2 his courage failed him in 1848 when he was put to the test by the
   authorities and seemed all too anxious to please (see Part 1 and

Chapter 6). His speech on Kennington Common when he urged the assembled masses 'in the name of courage, in the name of justice, in the name of God, not to hold the procession, and thus throw this great cause into the hands of pickpockets and scoundrels' was widely believed to be a humiliating betrayal.

Questions, therefore, still remain against Feargus O'Connor, but it cannot be denied that his reputation has stood higher in the last 20 years than ever before.

The other important historiographical development of the last 20 years has been against what might be called the 'Briggs' methodology which pictures Chartism as a series of interconnected, but essentially locally focused, episodes. The editors of a collection of important articles published in 1983 made their position clear:

◢ View 5

Chartism was not simply a political challenge, it was a challenge to authority and to doctrinaire ideology in a whole number of areas. Industrial action, cultural confrontation, resistance to domination from the pulpit as well as from employers and local and national government, were offered by working people in the Chartist movement at a whole number of different levels ... In all cases it was informed by a strong sense of class identity, a strong defence of working-class institutions and customs, and a pervasive belief in the importance and strength of democratic process, both at the level of local and national politics, and in the workplace and in the community.

*J. Epstein and D. Thompson (eds), **The Chartist Experience: Studies in Working-class Radicalism and Culture, 1830–60** (Macmillan, 1982)*

With this ringing statement of class identity in our ears, it seems ironic that what has proved to be the most influential article in the collection refused to portray Chartism like this. Gareth Stedman Jones believed that Chartism is best seen, not as the first working-class movement, but as a continuation of a rich vein of artisan-radical politics which had surfaced impressively at intervals since the English civil wars of the 1640s. The Chartist phase of radicalism in the 1830s and early 1840s, in Stedman Jones's view, was characterised by:

◢ a wish to persevere with a broad, popular alliance between radicals from different backgrounds to secure necessary political changes, rather than by new politics based on class hostility

◢ greater support from working people because the 1832 Reform Act had deliberately excluded them from the political process

◢ still greater opposition to a state which passed hostile legislation, such as the Poor Law Amendment Act of 1834 (see Chapter 1).

He also believed that Chartism lost impetus and vision in the early 1840s, considerably earlier than is suggested by most other late twentieth-century historians of Chartism.

Stedman Jones used a new ***methodology*** to understand what he saw as the essence of Chartism. The approach he favoured was a study of Chartist language divorced, as he put it, from its 'social inferences'. By this he meant that historians have made too many assumptions about the nature of Chartism based on knowledge of its social context – depressed handloom weavers, the early stages of industrialisation, the plight of factory workers and so on. For Stedman Jones, this knowledge has distorted reality. Instead, he looked to a study of Chartist language to 'establish a far closer and more precise relationship between ideology and activity than is conveyed in the standard picture of the movement.' His contribution fitted into an increasingly influential intellectual movement vaguely (and inadequately) called '***postmodernism***'.

◢ View 6

In contrast to the prevalent social-historical approach to Chartism, whose starting point is some conception of class … consciousness, [this article] argues that the ideology of Chartism cannot be constructed [outside] its linguistic form. An analysis of Chartist ideology must start from what Chartists actually said or wrote, the terms in which they addressed either each other or their opponents … If the interpretation of the language and politics is freed from [historical assumptions about the state of society] it then becomes possible to establish a far closer and more precise relationship between ideology and activity than is conveyed in the standard picture of the movement.

*G. Stedman Jones, 'The language of Chartism' in J. Epstein and D. Thompson (eds), **The Chartist Experience: Studies in Working-class Radicalism and Culture, 1830–60** (Macmillan, 1983)*

You can see from numbers 1–3 of the short-term causes identified in Chapter 1 what Stedman Jones was suggesting. Chartism for him was a continuation of an old radical tradition in new circumstances. This view was controversial enough in itself but his 'linguistic' methodology has proved even more so.

KEY TERMS

Methodology is the system of methods and rules used by someone studying a subject. In history writing, the methodology is often related to types of sources and to the way the historian uses them. Historians normally use a variety of sources from the period. Most of these are written, such as letters, books, speeches, but sources might include physical remains and visual sources, such as the architecture of buildings, inscriptions, portraits and cartoons. Relevant sources also include those written later, including the work of other historians. When historians criticise each other's methodology it is often on the basis of the sources used, their balance, their fitness for purpose and the weight which has been placed on them.

Postmodernism is a movement which attempts to go beyond 'modern' assumptions about values, attitudes and beliefs. Much influenced by scholars of language and philosophers, it argues that language cannot relate to anything except itself. In historical terms, therefore, such a view challenges the way historians relate sources both to one another and to a known context, coming to views about the relative importance of types of evidence and, thus, sustaining their own interpretations of the past. Postmodernists challenge the idea that any context can be certainly known; they also challenge any notions of 'objective evidence' or 'objective knowledge'. Some even claim that 'history' is nothing more than the invention of historians. This intellectual development has deeply disturbed some historians, who wonder what their subject is for. Many more have either ignored or disparaged it, arguing, in essence, that postmodernism is nothing more than the power of logic pushed beyond all reason. In other words, postmodernists lack common sense and are being silly.

A leading critic of Stedman Jones is Neville Kirk, who has made a detailed study of the factory districts of Lancashire and Cheshire. From his own study he reasserts that Chartism was indeed 'class-based' and vitally concerned with 'questions of poverty, exploitation, class relations and related issues'. His attack on Stedman Jones's views focuses on Stedman Jones's methodology:

◢ View 7

In short, [his] large generalisations are erected upon relatively slight, arguably insufficient, empirical foundations. In addition, it may be suggested that Stedman Jones offers a highly selective reading of his source material ... An alternative reading of the very same sources reveals an intensely class-based language, which was at the heart of Chartism.

N. Kirk, 'In defence of class' in **International Review of Social History**, vol. xxxii (1987)

Another historian, P.A. Pickering, has tried to play Stedman Jones at his own linguistic game, pointing out that he has not '*deconstructed*' his evidence enough. The reports of Chartist speeches, on which Stedman Jones places so much store, were usually selective. Furthermore, Feargus O'Connor, like so many gifted orators, relied for his impact upon interaction with the audience. Reports of his speeches miss so much of their true significance:

◢ View 8

Oratory should be set in a context of total performance ... the public meeting [was] an episode in which oratorical performance was only one aspect of communication. In fact, for some Chartists the speeches were of relatively little importance; at least this is the impression given at the massive Chartist gathering on Kersal Moor in September 1838 when, towards the end of the meeting, several speakers were interrupted in mid-sentence by various bands that struck up in preparation for the march home. Although someone like O'Connor and other leaders were probably treated with more reverence, even they could communicate orally at the massive meetings only with the small percentage of the audience able to obtain a position within earshot. At the ... meeting on Peep Green in May 1839, for example, the Northern Star *admitted that not even 10% of the vast crowd were able to hear'.*

P. A. Pickering, 'Class without words: Symbolic communication in the Chartist movement' in **Past and Present**, vol. 112 (1986)

Pickering urged us to understand both the ritual and the 'public theatre' aspects of Chartism as a means of revealing its true significance for ordinary people. Here an understanding of context helps us to see Chartism, in modern jargon, as a truly 'interactive' experience. Chartist meetings, then, were in part recreation – and fun! Whole families attended; children played while their parents listened, and reacted, to the speeches. All of this may have been an expression of 'class solidarity'; it was certainly a means of bonding and mutual support. It mattered, though understanding precisely *how* takes us into the realms of speculation. Chartism, the most thoroughly documented of all popular movements, still allows us direct access to frustratingly little about those below the level of local leadership. The functions and significance of those mass public meetings addressed by the national leaders may indeed have had more local, and specifically social and cultural, significance for the great majority who attended. To that extent at least, the attempt of the revisionist historians of the 1970s and 1980s to persuade us that (whether class-based or not) Chartism was, first and foremost, a national, political movement may need qualification. Perhaps Asa Briggs's 'localist' approach has more enduring validity than its many recent critics suppose.

Interpretations of Chartism have changed substantially in recent years, but where are we now? Towards the end of the 1990s, a brave attempt was made to argue that 'postmodern, *linguistic-turn*' and 'socialist-Marxist' historians have more in common than either group might suppose.

KEY TERMS

Structuralism is closely linked to postmodernism. It refers to study which regards any writing, or 'text', as a structure which is sufficient in itself and should be examined independent of its author or its intended audience. Getting to the allegedly 'pure' text involves a process of **'deconstruction'**, which involves scraping away all the layers of assumption about intrinsic merit or context.

Linguistic turn – a phrase used to describe the consequence of attention to structuralist ideas. Thus, historians who have taken the 'linguistic turn' have abandoned conventional means of weighing evidence according to context and have attempted to 'deconstruct' their evidence.

◢ View 9

Dorothy Thompson and Gareth Stedman Jones can be said to have reached a common point of departure for a revised approach to the study of Chartism. Both are sceptical about explanations of Chartism which emphasised its peculiar local or occupational character, both rejected the view that Chartism was simply a protest movement, whether of a backward-looking or proto-socialist kind and both were concerned to bring out the specifically political content of the movement ...

Both historians emphasise the rational nature of chartist arguments and ideas, stressing that this was an articulate popular movement based on a clearly defined set of political demands ... Both see chartism as a national movement, united by a common programme, a recognizable leadership and a widely disseminated popular press. This not only represents a break with the localism so characteristic of chartist studies in the 1960s, but also moves beyond an older preoccupation with the divisions within the chartist leadership ... Finally, neither account sees chartism as a spasmodic reaction to industrialisation or the trough in the trade cycle, or a backward-looking reaction to a new urban society.

*M. Taylor, 'Rethinking the Chartists' in **The Historical Journal**, vol. 39 (1996), pp484–85*

As a summary of the dominant historiographical position, it is difficult to disagree with much of this. Taylor's article, however, makes no attempt to assess whether newer interpretations which, among other things, rehabilitate Feargus O'Connor and emphasise Chartism as a potent national movement of working people to achieve radical political change are to be preferred over older ones which stressed Chartism's weaknesses and divisions and the desperation of much of its activity. Older views also suggest that most of what was good about Chartism came from its 'moral-force', improving artisans. Such views are now unfashionable but they may not be wrong. Newer does not necessarily mean better and those studying interpretations of Chartism need to make up their own minds on the basis of the evidence.

TASKS

Analysing interpretations

Either alone or in small groups, answer the following questions which are all about the way the Chartist movement and its leaders have been represented by historians:

Q1 *'Study View 1 (page 97).*
What, according to this source, is Gammage's opinion of Feargus O'Connor as a Chartist leader? Show how the content and language of the source emphasises the impression Gammage wishes to create.'

HINT: This question is in two parts. The first can be answered briefly: was Gammage a supporter of O'Connor or not? The second requires more thought. It's always important to distinguish between 'language' and 'content'. You can use skills of *comprehension* (see Tasks in Chapter 4, pages 92–94) to get a fair way on content. The language (and sometimes you are also asked to comment on 'tone', which relates to the overall impression a document gives rather than to individual instances of language) requires you to think about how the author uses particular words, or whole sentences, to convey an impression. The examiner here invites you to delve below the surface. In working on questions like this, therefore, it is very important to comment not only on the *matter* presented but also on the *manner* in which the impression is conveyed.

Q2 *'Study Views 1 and 2 (pages 97–100).*
Does Hovell agree with Gammage about Feargus O'Connor as a Chartist leader? Explain your answer by reference to both views.'

HINT: A straightforward statement of agreement or disagreement is unlikely to be sufficient. Look for different emphases and 'shades of grey' in the broader context of your answer.

Q3 *'Study Views 3, 4 and 5 (pages 101–103).*
In what ways, according to the evidence of these three views, do Epstein and Thompson's judgements about Chartism as a whole influence their assessment of the leadership of Feargus O'Connor?'

HINT: You must study all three sources. A good answer first requires you to judge what kind of a movement the two authors thought Chartism to be. From this base, you can relate their assessment of

O'Connor as a leader to their own views about what kind of leadership Chartism needed.

Q4 *'Study View 6 (page 104).*
What approaches to the history of Chartism is Stedman Jones attacking here and on what grounds?'

HINT: The key to answering this question lies in your understanding of how Stedman Jones believes Chartism should be studied. You will need more than the skill of comprehension to get to the answer: you need to *infer* as well. You can make use of the section immediately before View 6 which discusses his opinions on the nature of Chartism.

Q5 *'Study Views 6, 7 and 8 (pages 104–107).*
In what ways, and to what extent, do Kirk and Pickering agree about the reasons for their rejection of Stedman Jones's interpretation of Chartism?'

HINT: You do not need to repeat Stedman Jones's views again here, but you will need to look at the criticisms offered by Kirk and Pickering about both his methodology and his findings. You should plan your answer carefully. It may be a good strategy to list similarities and differences in Views 7 and 8 before coming to a final judgement about the 'extent' of overall agreement.

Q6 *'Study all the views and use your own knowledge.*
"Interpretations of Chartism have become more sophisticated and more valid as time has gone on. We now understand much more about the movement than was known before the 1950s."'

HINT: This is a huge question and perhaps not best tackled as an essay.

You may wish to set up a class debate with different individuals, or groups, being responsible for researching different aspects of it. Findings can then be reported and a discussion held before the different views are summarised in the form of a response to this controversial quotation.

CHAPTER SIX

WAS CHARTISM A FAILURE?

Objectives

◢ To examine in what senses Chartism 'failed' and in what senses it did not

◢ To analyse the extent, and nature, of the forces ranged against Chartism

◢ To understand the legacy of Chartism after 1848.

The Chartists never came near to achieving their famous 'Six Points' in the 1830s and 1840s. From the time of their first National Convention in 1839, the Chartists were divided about central questions such as how to react when parliament rejected their petition and how best to present their case for the vote. All attempts at direct action in 1839, 1840 and 1842 quickly ended in failure. Once they were over, the events of 10 April 1848 were widely interpreted by the authorities as a last, humiliating climb-down by a demoralised group whose bluff had been well and truly called (see Part 1). The intention of the cartoon on the following page from the humorous political magazine *Punch* was, of course, ridicule.

We should not be too swayed by hindsight. By no means all of the upper and middle classes took the Chartist threat lightly. For many, a revolutionary response from the British lower orders, similar to those which had overthrown or destabilised governments in Paris, Vienna, Berlin, Milan and Venice in February and March 1848, was very likely in London in April:

◢ Source 1

London is in a state of panic from the contemplated meeting of the Chartists, 200 000 strong on Monday ... The Times is alarmed beyond measure. I have it on good authority that the Chartists are determined to have their wishes granted.

> The nonconformist writer Garth Wilkinson, in a letter to his wife,
> 7 April 1848, quoted in D. Thompson, **The Chartists: Popular**
> **Politics in the Industrial Revolution** (Temple Smith, 1984)

The next day, two days before the Kennington Common meeting, Queen Victoria and other members of the royal family left London by train for the safety of Osborne House on the Isle of Wight. Only with

Figure 8 'A physical-force Chartist aiming for the fight'
Source: *Punch*

hindsight do we know that the meeting itself turned out to be a damp squib; some of the greatest in the land were far from convinced at the time that it would be.

Nevertheless, Chartism was not to threaten the authorities again. Dorothy Thompson quite correctly noted that 'As far as the achievement of the six points went, the Chartists failed completely.' (D. Thompson, *The Chartists*). So was Chartism itself a failure? The remainder of this chapter investigates this question. It also asks why Chartism ran out of steam after 1848 and looks briefly at what came out of Chartism. First, though, it is worth noticing what the Chartists were up against.

The power of the state

A very simple point about Chartism is often overlooked. It was faced by anti-democratic forces of overwhelming superiority. There are a number of reasons for this:

1 By the 1840s, the state had long experience of handling radical disaffection. It knew how to avoid creating martyrs, while also taking firm action when it felt it necessary. Home Secretaries (the government ministers responsible for public order) were well briefed about trouble spots both by civil servants and local magistrates (Justices of the Peace). The policy of arresting leading Chartists and imprisoning them for a year or two, as happened in 1839–40 and 1842–3, was usually very successful. It took the heat out of the situation.

2 Two new developments strengthened the power of the state still further:

   ◢ new professional police forces were being created under legislation passed for London in 1829 and the counties from 1839
   ◢ the 1830s and especially the 1840s were great decades of railway building. By 1840, 1 500 miles of track were open, linking most of Britain's large towns and cities with London. By 1850, 6 000 miles were open and a genuine railway network was available. This was important for a number of reasons. Not least,

it enabled the authorities to transport large numbers of troops to trouble spots much more easily than before:

◢ Source 2

You send a battalion of 1 000 men from London to Manchester [by rail] in nine hours: that same battalion marching would take 17 days; and they arrive at the end of nine hours just as fresh, or nearly so, as when they started.

> Evidence of an army Quartermaster to a parliamentary select committee
> on Railways, 1844, quoted in J. Saville, **1848: The British State and
> the Chartist Movement** (Cambridge University Press, 1987)

The railway companies could themselves help this process. The Lancashire and Yorkshire Railway Company enrolled 700 of their workmen as special constables in anticipation of public disorder in April 1848, for example, despite many workmen's great reluctance.

◢ Source 3

We are placed entirely under martial law, and the most absolute despotism is practised upon us.

> John Richards, reporting on the situation in the Potteries, Northern Star, 9 July 1842,
> quoted in R. Fyson, 'Homage to John Richards', in O. Ashton, R. Fyson and S. Roberts (eds),
> **The Duty of Discontent: Essays for Dorothy Thompson** (Mansell, 1995)

3 The British state was much more confident about the extent to which it represented 'propertied opinion' after 1832. The Reform Act of that year had given votes to the overwhelming majority of the middle classes and had produced a constituency system closer to the distribution of population and wealth than the one it replaced. A prime aim of the Whigs in passing that Bill had been to detach the middle classes from their dangerous alliance with working people. To a very large extent, their strategy succeeded. Most in the middle classes wanted to preserve public order and to consolidate their position in society, rather than to take on the aristocracy in a bid for more power. The increased influence of the middle classes in local government after the Municipal Corporations Act in 1835 provided further support for the

established regime. A government of landowners, therefore, could count on much more propertied support against the radicals in the early 1840s than in the early 1830s. Just before his arrest, John Richards wrote a letter to a friend which attributed the failure of the 1842 strike in the Potteries to the power of the state:

◢ **Source 4**

... when I reflect on the cause, and see the goodly Fabrick of Chartism thrown down in these parts, my Soul sinks within me and I feel completely unmann'd ... We are now in the midst of a Tory reign of terror. Spies and Informers are now the only persons who seem to be noticed, no matter what their Character may be.

John Richards to Joshua Hobson, 22 August 1842, quoted in
O. Ashton, R. Fyson and S. Roberts (eds), **The Duty of Discontent:**
Essays for Dorothy Thompson *(Mansell, 1995)*

4 State power was not always used oppressively. Some historians have pointed to the legislation passed in the 1840s which was designed, at least in part, to improve living and working conditions for the population. The repeal of the Corn Laws in 1846, though it failed to bring cheap bread to the masses as the Anti-Corn Law League had said it would, earned Sir Robert Peel great praise from many working-class leaders. Historians of Chartism tend not to notice how much popular sympathy the death of the arrogant and aloof Conservative prime minister after a riding accident in 1850 caused among ordinary people. Peel died almost a popular hero.

In the 1840s also, both Peel's Conservative government and the Whig government of Lord John Russell which succeeded it in 1846 passed legislation which imposed closer regulation of women and children in mines and factories. In 1847, workers won their maximum 'ten-hour' working day. Though conditions in workhouses remained dreary and unpleasant, some of the roughest edges of the New Poor Law were smoothed by legislation in 1846 and 1847, and 1848 saw the passage of the first Public Health Act. Peel's Bank Charter Act of 1844 also helped to bring much-needed stability into financial markets, reducing the likelihood of damaging 'crashes' producing bankruptcies and widespread unemployment. Some historians argue that these initiatives amounted to little for most working people and that their intentions were not primarily benevolent anyway. It is difficult to deny, however, that, by 1850, the worst excesses of deprivation and depression were over or that governing classes had shown a desire to escape the old charge that they only passed legislation which advantaged a privileged few. In this context, the repeal of the Corn Laws had a symbolic significance which exceeded its practical short-term effects.

Why did Chartism decline?

It is common ground among historians that the Chartists did not threaten the authorities after 1848. Recent historiography has tended to suggest that 1848 itself represented a greater challenge than used to be thought and some kind of organisation was indeed maintained for another decade (see Chronology of important events, page 7), but the fact of sharp overall decline is incontestable.

Why this decline occurred, however, has been the subject of considerable debate. Among the main factors which have received attention are:

1 Argument:	Counter-argument:
The end of the severe economic depressions which had brought the masses out on to the streets in protest.	Although severe depressions such as those experienced in 1839 and 1842 did disappear, it is difficult to prove that living standards among working people as a whole increased significantly until the 1870s and 1880s.

2 Argument:

Governments were more attuned to the 'social question' than before and began to pass legislation designed to reduce social tension and class hostility (see page 116). The changing nature of the British state, and its growing self-confidence during a period of economic boom, were major factors in the fragmentation of Chartism.

Counter-argument:

The amount of legislation designed to improve conditions was limited and legislation had little practical effect. The New Poor Law remained a symbol of degradation and disgrace which humiliated those who needed to use it. State confidence is anyway easily exaggerated, as the great soul-searching which took place over Britain's early failures in the Crimean war (1854–56) demonstrated.

3 Argument:

O'Connor's credibility was shattered by his climb-down in 1848 and this led to further disputes among Chartist leaders and disillusionment among followers.

Counter-argument:

Although O'Connor's powers were waning, there were other leaders (notably Ernest Jones and Bronterre O'Brien) who remained vigorous and committed. They also had a clear agenda.

4 Argument:

The three great efforts made in 1838–39, 1841–42 and 1848 had all failed. After such reverses, there was no stomach for further mass agitation or revolutionary preparation.

Counter-argument:

Some of those Chartists, such as the followers of Bronterre O'Brien, who remained committed to the cause were as revolutionary as any nineteenth-century political leaders. They joined socialist and other extreme radical groups in Europe with the aim of creating a genuinely international **proletarian** revolution.

KEY TERM

Proletarian – this word was extensively used by Marxist historians to include unskilled and semi-skilled workers whose only means of survival was selling their labour. According to Marxist theory, given the right leadership and appropriate economic conditions, these workers would rise up and seize power from the middle classes.

5 Argument:

Economically depressed skilled workers, especially the handloom weavers, had always been at the centre of Chartist agitation. Their numbers were now declining very quickly. In 1840, they numbered approximately 123 000; by 1850 their numbers were down to 43 000. By 1860, they had all but disappeared in most areas. With them went the motive force of Chartism.

Counter-argument:

We should not exaggerate the importance of one working group. Other skilled workers remained and could have revived Chartism as a mass threat if other conditions had been right.

6 Argument:

Chartism was betrayed by the *aristocracy of labour*. Those who had supported Chartism during the late 1830s and 1840s were frustrated by lack of success and looked to other organisations – trade unions, co-operative and friendly societies, other self-help groups, even the parliamentary Liberal party – to advance their interests. Without their active co-operation, Chartism was bound to wither.

Counter-argument:

This exaggerates the importance of one, fairly small, group of workers. In any case, many members of this group had not been among Chartism's strongest supporters in the 1840s. Their defection, therefore, was of limited importance to a working-class organisation.

KEY TERM

Aristocracy of labour – usually referred to as the working-class elite: skilled workers who had more secure jobs and higher rates of pay. Many of them joined trade unions which protected their interests. In one version of Marxist theory, the aristocracy of labour should have led the proletarians into working-class revolution. However, in Britain during the late 1840s and 1850s, many of these skilled workers saw the benefits of working within, rather than against, the capitalist system. Some Marxist historians believed that this was why the world's first industrial nation failed to generate the world's first working-class revolution.

Clearly, the evidence does not point all one way. It is also interesting how often historians with different political views stress similar factors. Thus, those strongly sympathetic to working-class political organisation stress the power of the state as an important reason why the Chartists did not achieve more. Those who resist class-based analyses also point to a more self-confident government's adoption of *laissez-faire* policies as the key to long-term growth and, thus, the decline of mere 'protest' movements. Similarly, even those keenest to rehabilitate Feargus O'Connor (see Chapter 3) as the vital force which united Chartism from 1840 onwards recognise that both his own powers and his political influence took a fatal knock in 1848.

For this author, the later history of Chartism provides further evidence of divergence, rather than unity. Chartism never had any realistic chance of success anyway, given the Whigs' ability to secure a substantial portion of middle-class allegiance to the old order by the 'Great' Reform Act of 1832 (see Part 1 and Chapter 1). Chartist demonstrations of collective support were immensely impressive on one level but most of its own leaders recognised that they were powerless against the concerted efforts of a powerful, and increasingly confident, government. A combination of sustained economic revival and declining political will (exacerbated by more or less continual disagreements over strategy and tactics) was sufficient to see off the Chartist threat by the end of the 1840s. Perhaps we should be more impressed, not by the sudden collapse of Chartism after 1848 (in many areas – notably central Scotland, south Wales and Staffordshire – it had been in full retreat from 1842 onwards), but by the intelligence, dedication and resource which kept it alive for so long in so many places.

Conclusion: *Was* Chartism a failure?

One final question remains to consider. Because Chartism did not achieve the 'Six Points', does that mean that it achieved nothing? Surely that would be too harsh a view. Particularly in the industrial areas of Lancashire and Yorkshire, Chartism was vital to the development of a distinctive culture among working people. This culture was complex, but some aspects of it seem clear. Out of Chartism came:

◢ at the very least scepticism, and usually hostility, towards a state which united the interests of the propertied middle and upper classes against those of working people. This was a vital legacy of 1832; pressure for factory reforms, against the New Poor Law and, above all, for the People's Charter all bore witness to it. For some Chartists, it is true, the state was opposed because it continued to represent (in very changed circumstances) the 'Old Corruption' of the pre-1832 era. For others, it was the *increased* state power after 1832 which was the main cause of discontent. Chartism accommodated both views

◢ from this scepticism, a fierce determination to pursue interests independently. This involved a number of objectives – educational, moral, temperance, Christian, trade union, etc. – which were not always mutually compatible. Chartism, however, provided the essential focus

◢ specific lessons in how to formulate protests, how to organise and how to spread the message of dissent. These lessons were not forgotten whatever the later direction which older Chartists took. The numerous autobiographies from the later nineteenth century confirm the importance of Chartism in working-class lives. The son of a handloom weaver – like so many – blamed 'physical force' but, interestingly, also asserted the benefits that the movement brought:

◢ Source 5

The Chartist movement was one to which all social and political reformers look back with a certain amount of pride, mingled with a great amount of sadness. Pride, because it was a movement inspired by great ideals; because it called forth a spirit of devotion and self-sacrifice which is rare in public movements and caught up on its 'moral-force side' some of the finest and most thoughtful working-class men of that time. Sadness, because its ideals were either shattered, or passed on ... into other movements and other parties; because its spirit of devotion and self-sacrifice was broken by brutal persecution and imprisonment; and because its 'moral force' was largely neutralised, and its adherents deluded and misled, by one or two inordinately vain and self-seeking agitators.

Ramsden Balmforth, 'Some social and political pioneers of the nineteenth century', quoted in E. Royle, **Chartism** (Addison Wesley Longman, 1996)

The divisions implied here continued after 1848. Some ex-Chartists moved into socialism; others moved into, or back into, trade unionism. Others again agitated for temperance reform as the key to unlock the potential of the working man. Vincent and Lovett remained sturdy working-class educators to the end – slightly bemused, perhaps, that there were so many who apparently spurned lessons for life and refused to adopt 'Sunday best' behaviour the whole week through. Many ex-Chartists found the mid-nineteenth-century Liberal party a surprisingly accommodating institution as its Whig leaders saw political advantage in encouraging a radical wing which no longer looked to pull down the pillars of the state. 'Liberal radicalism' became an increasingly influential force in the 1850s and 1860s. From it came renewed cries for parliamentary reform which would be answered (though hardly in the way that they had anticipated) by an opportunistic Benjamin Disraeli and the Conservatives in 1867. It is worth noting both that the famous 'new model unions' of skilled craftsmen were strong supporters of parliamentary reform and that they were adept at threatening strike action and occasionally acting on that threat when they judged it would benefit their members. Political and industrial objectives rarely came unstitched after Chartism.

Chartists after 1848, then, took different routes. In the much studied textile and engineering centre of Oldham, for example, some ex-Chartists who had co-operated with the Tory humanitarian John Fielden during his factory reform campaigns grew closer to the Conservative party because, as the Oldham delegate to the 1848 convention asserted, the *laissez-faire* ideology of Liberals and Peelites was 'the most heartless and destructive doctrine ever taught in any country' (D. Gadian, 'Radicalism and Liberalism in Oldham' *Social History*, vol. 21 (1996)). Others moved happily enough into Liberal radicalism. The records of the weaver-dominated Chartist branch of the

National Charter Association in Great Horton (Bradford) survive from
1840 until 1866, by which time it had changed into a very different
organisation. In the 1860s and 1870s, it embraced the co-operative
movement and Liberal radicalism (D. G. Wright, *Popular Radicalism*,
Longman, 1988).

Whatever the divergence and the disagreements, one key point must
be stressed: Chartism marked them all. It left a permanent legacy of
independence, resource and often cussed bloody-mindedness. David
Jones's assessment catches both the essence of Chartism and why, for
so many, it continued to matter for up to a half-century after 1848:

◢ Source 6

*The history of Chartism after [O'Connor's] fall from power revealed ... that each person
had his own order of priorities, his own definition of freedom, and his own views of the
relationship between power and knowledge and between the individual and the state.
For this reason Chartists reacted differently to the economic and political progress of
the mid-Victorian era. Some settled down to an Advanced Liberalism; some moved into
independent Labour politics, and others retired in confusion and bitterness. But almost
all of them retained that tough and independent spirit which had made them
'Irreconcilables'.*

D. Jones, **Chartism and the Chartists** (Allen Lane, 1975)

Individual or group activity

Below are two hypotheses about Chartism. Using the evidence in this book, and any other information you have, discuss the strengths and weaknesses of both. Then decide which of them provides the more valid judgement overall.

Hypothesis A

Chartism faced overwhelming odds, yet was able to chalk up many successes. Though it did not achieve the 'Six Points', it gave working people organisation, direction and confidence. It was a long-term success.

Hypothesis B

Chartism attempted too much. It underestimated the power of the forces ranged against it and its failures led to division and demoralisation. Meanwhile, working people looked to other organisations to protect their interests.

Hints on procedure

These two hypotheses ask you to investigate some big questions. You will find material relevant to them in all of the chapters in this book. It would be sensible, for each hypothesis, to draw up lists divided into two columns. Select evidence in support of the hypothesis in one column, and against it in the other. For each piece of evidence, note down the chapter and page number. This will help you to cross-refer when you come to consider the two hypotheses together at the end of the exercise. A final question: are these two hypotheses total opposites, or are there ways in which they can be reconciled? Explain your answer.

FURTHER READING

Chartism has generated a vast literature. The purpose of the guide
which follows is to lead readers to other relevant works. The list below
should be sufficient for most A-level and AS students who are studying
the topic. It does not attempt to provide students who may be writing
a personal study, or similar extended piece of writing, with a
comprehensive bibliography. For this, readers are referred to the works
cited in the bibliographies of Royle and Walton under the 'General
Studies of Chartism' section below.

Introductory studies

H. Browne, *Chartism* (Access to History, Hodder and Stoughton, 1999)

H. Cunningham   'The nature of Chartism' in *Britain 1815–67*
(Heinemann, 1994), pp51–57 – a collection of essays which first
appeared in the sixth-form journal *Modern History Review*, vol. 4
(1990)

E. J. Evans, 'Chartism revisited' in *History Review*, vol. 33 (1999)

E. J. Evans   *The Birth of Modern Britain, 1780–1914* (Addison Wesley
Longman, 1997) – pp147–55 of this A-Level text assume no prior
knowledge of the movement

E. Royle   'The origins and nature of Chartism' in *History Review*,
vol. 13 (1990)

General studies of Chartism

O. Ashton, R. Fyson and S. Roberts (eds)   *The Duty of Discontent: Essays
for Dorothy Thompson* (Mansell, 1995) – chapters 1–4 are relevant

J. Belchem   *Popular Radicalism in Nineteenth-century Britain* (Macmillan,
1996) – chapter 5 concentrates on Chartism

A. Briggs (ed)   *Chartist Studies* (Macmillan, 1959) – a series of essays
concentrating mostly on Chartism in particular localities

R. Brown, *Chartism* (Cambridge University Press, 1998)

J. Charlton   *The Chartists* (Pluto, 1997) – brief and highly sympathetic
class-based treatment

J. Epstein and D. Thompson (eds)   *The Chartist Experience: Studies in
Working-class Radicalism and Culture, 1830–60* (Macmillan, 1982) – a
collection inspired by the need to see Chartism as an integrated
national movement and not merely as a series of local experiences.

E. Royle *Chartism*, 3rd edition (Addison Wesley Longman, 1996) – the best detailed introduction; it also has a good selection of documents and an excellent bibliography

J. K. Walton *Chartism* (Lancaster Pamphlet, 1999) In part a reaction to the Briggs collection above. Includes the influential article on 'Languages of Chartism' by G. Stedman Jones

E. Royle *Chartism*, 3rd edition (Addison Wesley Longman, 1996) – the best introduction to the subject, with a good selection of documents

D. Jones *Chartism and the Chartists* (Allen Lane, 1975) – remains the best thematic account

M. Taylor 'Rethinking the Chartists: Searching for synthesis in the historiography of Chartism' in *Historical Journal*, vol. 39 (1996) – as its title implies, this is not an easy read. It is, however, by some distance the best summary of where debates on Chartism had got to by the mid-1990s

D. Thompson *The Chartists: Popular Politics in the Industrial Revolution* (Temple Smith, 1984) – in effect a series of highly engaged, well-researched essays portraying Chartism as a political and cultural movement with deep roots in class consciousness

J. T. Ward *Chartism* (Batsford, 1973) – a narrative account. Reliable for factual information but lacking analytical insight in places and now rather out of date

D. G. Wright *Popular Radicalism: The Working-class Experience, 1780–1880* (Longman, 1988) – chapters 5 and 6 are relevant

Specific themes and approaches

Biographical studies

J. Epstein *The Lion of Freedom* (Croom Helm, 1982) – major attempt to rescue O'Connor from an undeservedly low reputation. Ends, frustratingly, in 1842

J. Saville *Ernest Jones, Chartist* (Lawrence and Wishart, 1952)

A. R. Schoyen *The Chartist Challenge* (Heinemann, 1958) – a biography of George Julian Harney

J. Wiener *William Lovett* (Manchester University Press, 1989)

D. Williams *John Frost: A Study in Chartism* (Evelyn, Adams and Mackay, 1969)

Chartist biographies

B. Harrison and P. Hollis (eds) *Robert Lowery: Radical and Chartist*

(Europa Publications, 1979)

W. Lovett *Life and Struggles* (Garland, 1984) – originally published 1876

J. Saville (ed) *The Life of Thomas Cooper* (Leicester University Press, 1971) and a new edition of autobiography first published 1872

Collections of documents

R. Brown and C. Daniels (eds) *The Chartists* (Macmillan, 1984)

P. Hollis (ed) *Class and Conflict in Nineteenth-century England, 1815–50* (Routledge, 1973) – chapters 12–17 focus entirely on Chartism

F. C. Mather (ed) *Chartism and Society* (Bell and Hyman, 1980)

R. F. Taylor (ed) *The Age of Peel* (University of Cambridge Local Examinations Syndicate, 1995) – theme 5 'Extra-parliamentary activity', pp101–30, provides some useful Chartist sources

D. Thompson (ed) *The Early Chartists* (Macmillan, 1971) – good introduction and commentary

INDEX

KEY TERMS

PROFILES

MAIN INDEX